HANSI & GREYLING

TIMOTHY F. NUGENT

Hansi and Greyling
© Timothy F Nugent, 2023

Edited & Published by Rebel Magic Book
www.rebelmagicbooks.com

ISBN: 9798870761015

REBEL
MAGIC
BOOKS

One

They didn't have a clue.

These coiffed, helmet-haired 'ladies who lunch' desecrating my holy of holies. They didn't know the history of this place. This sanctum sanctorum. The one place on the planet where I found solace, comfort, knowledge, connection. My year of studying abroad had been rooted in this place.

I picked my jaw off the ground and tripped across the cobles worn back to Roman times to verify I had the right place. The name, correct. The date of founding – 1878 – chiseled in stone above the door where a knot of the hoitie-toitie of Salzburg were triple kissing greetings and ooh-ing and ah-ing about seafood salads, medallions of venison, and luscious white wines they'd be downing until teatime.

Something akin to disgust shuddered through me.

I returned here for this?

I dropped my luggage at the hotel then retraced by memory the route through the hustle and bustle of Altstadt for this?

From Maxglan, through the tunnel and Universitatsplatz, onto Getreidegasse until I reached the footbridge that still bounced with every step. To find that it had all changed?

It wasn't disgust. I was incredulous.

My dark, brooding, politics-infested pub had morphed into a Weinstube.

The insult was not enough to keep me out though.

I hefted myself up the stairs to enquire about a table for one and received the look of shame for being single and, Valkyrie forbid, alone. The maitresse'd led me up the stairs past 'my table' to the Wagnerian heights. I had a quick reminisce about sharing the weights of philosophy, politics, and social concerns with local students and young faculty from the university. She seated me with a view of the joint, from where I further remembered the comings and goings of gay men and the conversations that altered my worldview forever.

As the only male on site, I fended the stares and glares, wondering if my pub was now a lesbian establishment meant for the olding debutantes of the elite class I had encountered at the Vienna Opera Ball years ago. The only time in my life when I hobnobbed with wealth and royalty for the only evening of my life that the rich and famous deigned to be in my humble yet awestruck presence. I danced among them. Our elbows touched. I waltzed over their feet. They glared and stared, conjuring me and my fellow students out of their Valhalla.

I felt it all again as I hunched over a wilted salad and sipped a flavorless wine.

After lunch, I touristed back across the Salzach to Mülln and the infamous Augustiner Bräu for an honest immersion back into the life I'd lived for one memorable year. I sat in the monastic garden with two liters of bier that quenched my disappointment to the point that I knew my trudge back to Maxglan and my hotel would be an adventure. Failing to empty my bladder in the Abbey pissoir, as I had done with male friends too many times before, I found the same wall that seemed stained with more than my piss. Shame kicked in at this point because I was always the prude in our student group who admonished others for the same stunt. The difference was that it was always dark when we stumbled toward our lodgings. I was sure no one was the wiser in broad daylight.

I had forgotten how quiet this part of the city was. I listened to the buzz of insects I couldn't see, the meowing of cats on the other side of the wall, and dogs yapping from inside the house across the street as I splashed Augustiner's out, announcing to anyone that an uncivilized American tourist was here.

For whatever reason, I didn't feel like a tourist. It was all familiar. Homey. Unrushed. Human-scaled. The way it was as a student – at least after the first few weeks of greeting the same shopkeepers, bankers, and local Polizei, who kept a keen eye out for drunken students from the good old US of A.

The late afternoon shone over the Alps, highlighting the Untersberg with its massif shadow and rays of golden light shooting over Salzburg toward the east. I paused at the corner of Neutorstrasse and Hübnergasse to get my bearings. Traffic was not as it was in the past because the city had routed non-locals to the river or west of Monchsberg, the crescent-shaped hill with the famous castle on one end and the modern art museum near the other end. The Siegmundstor tunnel was not so heavily used now except to access parking or to walk into Altstadt, which is what I had done after I dropped my luggage at the hotel and waded through jetlag to my pub-cum-Weinstube.

It was too early to return to the hotel and walking around the neighborhood of my youth would help with the jetlag. I meandered through Maxglan to see what establishments survived the intervening years and to plan a few walks over the coming days. It is not a long distance to anywhere on this side of the Monchsberg. In a couple of minutes, I stood, still wavering from my biers, across the street from the building that was central to our student life. It was in this grey-stuccoed, early twentieth century former private home where we studied, ate our meals, and socialized with each other.

After observing the Center for a short while, with no one entering or leaving, I was about to cross the Strasse to ring the chime. I looked both directions but didn't see the gentleman approaching from the Altstadt direction.

"Verzeihung. Kann Ich Ihnen helfen?" the man said, standing far enough away to not intrude but close enough to be heard clearly.

"Ich gut, danke," I replied hastily in my American-accented, Austrian-tinged facsimile of German. I looked both ways again but as my right foot hit the street pavement, a hand gripped my arm and pulled me back.

"Greyling. You haven't changed."

For a second time in four hours, my jaw struck the ground, this time confused that someone would know me. It flashed through my bier-addled brain that an attendant from Augustiner's followed me because I hadn't paid properly. I knew I hadn't nicked a crockery stein as a souvenir, which I had done too many times in the past. I couldn't work out who had a vice grip pulling me back to the sidewalk.

"Leider, wo sind Sie? And why am I to do what you want?" My touristischer pique popped out of my mouth as I shook the man's grip away.

His thunderous laugh entered and left my head in a tsunami of recognition.

"Hansi? Es du?"

"You have got to stop pissing on people's walls, Greyling. You aren't nineteen years old anymore, at least that seems the case from your inability to hold your bier."

My confusion clearly showed on my face.

"I was with friends at Augustiner's," he said. "Only old men drink alone there. I am sorry we have become so old."

I ran my hands over my face, stimulating some coherence.

"What are you doing here? I mean—here on this spot. I knew you could be living in Salzburg. I—. Can we—. What the fuck is happening?"

His chortle was more like an insult than a response to my lack of humor.

"You never came back." His words cut into me with precision. A scalpel rent me from my grey hair to my aching big toes.

"I wrote."

"Yes—and never came back."

"Hansi, my life changed. It stopped making sense. I tried to tell you. I threw a lot of letters away unsent. After a while it didn't make sense to keep trying. It was all different."

His harrumph cut deeper. Its dismissiveness reminded me of his frequent repudiations of my limited worldview, my stymied experience, my guarded curiosity of those long-ago years. It also awakened memories of why he and I were so delighted with each other, willing to listen, question, and harangue in ways that changed both of us at the time.

"How many of my letters did you throw away? Probably unread because of your fear. How many days did you wonder about me and what we had planned?" he asked.

"Can we not do this, Hans. Please? It's so long ago."

He turned toward Sigmundstor or back toward Augustiner Bräu. I begged my brain to de-fog so I could think what to do or say.

"I'm at our hotel," I dithered in shame.

He turned back. "At least it is no longer a flop house."

"I think I will shift to a better one in Altstadt."

I watched his familiar stride until he turned left onto Hübnergasse, wondering who his friends were and if I'd see him again.

I glanced across to the Center, shrugged, then turned toward Altstadt. As I passed Hübnergasse I saw him, still in his alpine hiking stride, disappearing in the distance. I waited until he was gone from view before trundling through the tunnel into town.

The top of Getreidegasse was always a thrill. Looking down the postcard-perfect lane filled with antique signs of wrought iron beauty never disappointed. The gentle wending of shops and apartments restored to historic perfection was a delight. The masses of humans devouring pastries, a joy.

The memories collided with others of Hansi. Hans Stepan Wortmann.

I slapped my face with both hands to reorder my thoughts. I stutter-stepped my way down Getreidegasse, seeking distraction but finding annoyance at myself and the stupid, arrogant, mostly American tourists whose lack of manners and respect for a different culture intruded to the point of anger. I shouted, in German to hide my shame of association, at a gaggle of midwestern numb nuts blocking the way. The shock on their faces and my physical belligerence achieved the effect I wanted and that I assumed others enjoying their day out also wanted, which meant they crunched together against a wall mumbling about how rude the locals are and that they should appreciate tourists more.

I smiled at achieving local status in less than a day, if only from midwestern ignoramuses. Perhaps by the time I've left in a few weeks I'd have convinced a real local or two, if not Hansi and his friends.

Carving my way through smaller streets to avoid more tourist encounters, I decided that being smack in the middle of old town wouldn't cut it, so I searched behind the baroque cathedral until I found a perfect hotel to transfer to. The concierge was kind enough to contact 'our hotel'—the one Hansi and I frequented when passion overrode our conversations—to arrange for my checkout and transfer of luggage, which fortunately I had not unpacked. I requested he have the other hotel tell anyone who asked about my new location. Hope might be the last great despair, but I decided I'd chance despair and posit hope into the universe, concepts I knew Hansi would ridicule and admonish.

I needed a quick refresh and sobering. I climbed the stairs to my room that included with the price a fantastic view of Hohensalzburg and the bluest cobalt of a sky I had seen in decades. Alpine air clears the skies and the mind. I kept the window open when I left.

In honor of embarrassing myself with Hansi, I decided to splurge on my first dinner of this trip. I scooted my way to the Nonntal district searching for a particular family-owned Gasthaus I'd discovered in my internet reminiscing, which had stood in for preparing my actual return. This one was billed as 'expecting a Michelin star any day now' sort of place. Just below a star was at the extreme top of my budget so I knew I'd be dining on bosna burgers and crepes for a couple of days. It was helpful that Frühstück was included in my room payments. If need be, I could have a full breakfast and squirrel a few yoghurts and Brot for a snack.

The Fräulein who greeted me smiled knowingly when I said I was dining alone. I wasn't sure what she thought she knew. Perhaps that my wife had died. Perhaps because single old men needed a knowing smile to feel comfortable dining alone in Salzburg. No matter, I accepted her smile with my own, which I feared might be interpreted as leering or as a misogynistic longing for companionship. I followed her into the garden to a table near the corner which kept me away from couples and four-top tables, but funneled traffic noises highlighted with whiffs of exhaust and diesel fumes right at me. Ah well. I was happy to be here, be seated, and being waited on by a smartly dressed, ever-so-Sound of Music Kurt-looking young gentleman. My leer couldn't have been too obvious when he brushed the back of my hand as he presented the menu.

I wrote my review of the place on an app for such things before the Strudel mit Schlag was served. You gotta have Strudel at least once when in Austria. The other delights would pile on over successive meals, starting with breakfast. My five-star review would win Kurt and his family the Michelin recognition they deserved, and if they awarded family members prizes for the best reviews my more than able server would win Steins down.

As I finished my dessert and the complimentary plum Schnapps, marveling that Kurt knew my preference without a word, I bid my aufwiedersehens and my bis spatters, deciding I'd dine here again on my last night before flying out.

The evening was darkening because the Untersberg and adjacent peaks of the Alps hid most remaining light from the west. With quaintness guiding my path, I sought out a bar I had seen near the Steingasse that proudly flew a rainbow flag over its door and had added a pink triangle to its historic coat of arms, probably in violation of city code. Clearly no one cared because it had been there for some time.

Steamy, biery, male odor danced in my nostrils. I always warmed to the smell of gay bars. Welcoming, familiar the world over, and still enough out of the ordinary to entice small amounts of danger into my brain, gay establishments awakened me from my meal, suggesting opportunity and family of my own. Being alone here did not include smirks or unknowing glances. Singleness is an acceptable, celebrated life choice in my community. No assumptions made. No expectations laid at feet.

Plenty of acknowledgments and enticing glances shot my way as I found a tall stool at the far end of the bar where I could survey the activity of men night-capping before heading home or to the home of a trick. I was content to accept that I would trundle back to my hotel by myself. The audience here was way too young for my tastes and appetites.

The single malt came with a couple of fingers of depth added above the two I had ordered. I acknowledged my gratitude with a much larger Euro note to ensure additional proper service should the occasion arise beyond what would clearly be another few hours of drunkenness after recovering from Augustiner's.

I pushed the reminder of Hansi into the black forest of my mind.

What popped to the fore was my recent memories of back home and what had prompted my return to Salzburg.

Thomas.

Thomas was the reason I had stopped writing to Hansi.

I ruminated through ten sips of scotch finally admitting that Hansi was an adult even back then and would have understood that I had met someone else. I owed him that explanation if I were to see him again.

Thomas swept me off my feet, probably because Hansi had opened my heart with his kindness, intelligence, and lovemaking. It was all new to me back then. I had learned from the best.

I learned even more from the second best.

Thomas meandered through my thoughts with the zing of scotch slipping down my throat. Each memory easier to swallow. Each ounce of pain warming me.

Maudlin is not something I do, much less reveal on my face. But I went there. I togged it up to jetlag and booze. I didn't cry but I could have.

Thomas.

Dead Thomas.

Dead after thirty years of love Thomas.

I felt the glory of it all bounce through my major organs. The emptiness of his death gurgled through the rest of me. I sat back on my stool, leaning against the wall. I caught my breath sucking the stale bar air in reminding me of where I was, telling myself I could wallow tomorrow during my walk to the top of Kapuzinerberg. I could wallow with the earthy fragrances, bird song, and the light of clear skies filtering through the aspens, larches, and ancient oaks.

I awoke from my vapors as the bartender topped me up with three more fingers. He pointed to Kurt standing at the other end of the bar with a few friends. I wagged two fingers his direction in gratitude and took a sip, knowing I should not try to down this generosity and should leave now—dignity and pride intact.

Kurt approached. I took a drag of air along with another sip.

"Thank you for your generous review," he said in school taught English. "My father and mother were very pleased."

"Were you pleased?" I asked with a tad too much tartiness.

Kurt laughed.

"Sam Greyling." I offered my American grip.

"Reinhardt," Kurt offered back.

"My apologies. I had it in my head that your name was Kurt. Sound of Music?"

"Ja. I get that from Americans. I have never seen the film."

"Julie Andrews is big in the States," I attempted to cover my ass in the gayest way I could muster.

"What brings you to Salzburg, Herr Greyling?"

"Nostalgia, most assuredly," I smiled through another imbibe.

"This is the town for it. Especially for Americans."

"You don't seem to like us, Herr Reinhardt."

He laughed through a swig of Stiegl Bier, the local standout brew.

"You are everywhere. Here. Vienna. Summer. Winter. It seems like Salzburg is more American than Austrian."

"Except for the language, food, music, beauty, and history. Yeah, Salzburg reminds me of Casper, Wyoming."

"I don't know what Casper, Wyoming is."

"Neither do they," the cheek of it. "I am sorry to keep you from your friends."

"You want me to leave?"

"No. I want to not bore you with my American ways and my American nostalgia. Is Reinhardt your first or last name?" My spirits-addled brain needed clarity on that.

"First," he said.

My eyebrows enquired further.

"Reinhardt Zecha. I thought you'd figured that out from the name of our restaurant. It's on the sign outside, on the menus, the plates, the crystal, the bierdeckeln, our uniforms." By now he was laughing. "You said you found us online, so I assumed you read the page with our history. Am I assuming that you are like many other Americans who pass through here?"

"Ignorant? Self-absorbed? Please don't tell me I am rude on top of that!"

"You said it, Herr Greyling." His smile waned.

"Well, Herr Reinhardt Zecha, I should go before I embarrass myself further. I plan to return to your restaurant so perhaps I will see you again before I depart for the America I know and mostly love."

Against all common sense and with my walk over the bouncing Salzach bridge looming, I downed two fingers of single malt. I stood, steadied myself on the bar, and took my first step.

"I'll walk you where you are going," Reinhardt said. "Where are you going?" His smile warmed me more than the scotch.

"Your friends?"

"They'll understand."

"They'll also assume."

"Naturlich." The cheek of it.

We broke into a huge American style laugh. Everyone turned to look then shouted "Prost" while raising their drinks in toast.

As we walked by his friends, Reinhardt said he'd see them at the party. They clapped me on the back and kissed him goodnight. They were a pleasant bunch of guys. I figured I wouldn't see them again.

"When's the last time you went to a gay party, Herr Greyling?"

We stood on the bridge. I begged him not to bounce.

"It does that on its own."

My curiosity bounced back for a minute, "What party is this?"

"Saturday night. Friends are going to the Festspielhaus, then I am meeting them after work. I thought you might like to come along."

"As you can see by my current state, I am not sure I am the partying type anymore."

"There will be mature men. You might even hook up for an Austrian adventure while you are here."

He walked me to the door of my hotel.

"You know where I am staying. Leave the address. Do I need to RSVP? This rude American prefers to be proper."

"I'll tell the host to expect another. If you don't come, I'll be disappointed and might be rude to you when you return to dine with us."

"Reinhardt, you could never be rude. You are much kinder than Kurt or Julie Andrews could ever be."

He turned to go, releasing my inebriated, jetlagged grip.

"You Americans!"

Two

Hansi was right. I couldn't hold my booze.

I got out of bed at 10:00, missing the included-in-the-price Frühstück. Wasted precious mountain water drenching myself in the shower trying to sweat the toxins out of me. Dressed by 11:15. I wandered to the river to find coffee and pastries, along with two glasses of orange juice, three rashers of bacon, and two poached eggs. Keeping it simple.

Fortified until lunch, I meandered back to the Steingasse stumbling around until I found the entry to Kapuzinerberg. Somehow my head got turned around and I kept trying to find my way through the same alley that I used to piss in when too drunk to get back to our student lodgings.

That memory got me thinking about the many nights at my pub. The Berg was covered in its summer canopy of leaves, with midday light streaking through the many species of trees, creating the illusion of heaven found in so many baroque paintings. As I ascended, I recalled one University of Salzburg student. I struggled to pull his name out of my memory banks, but I could see him clearly gesticulating as if shooing flies away from his head. I could hear his baritone rumbling in our nook about the United States' neo-colonial approach to Vietnam and to Latin American countries before that. He dismissed Korea as the Soviet's neo-colonial encroachment to provoke and distract the West from the murderous internal oppression by Stalin and then Khruschchev and Brezhnev, and the insertion of China onto the world stage by the neo-communist, fascistic Mao and his klan, spelled with a gesticulated 'k' to make a point to his American audience of one. I marveled like a second grader that anyone could know so much about global geopolitics and have cogent opinions like a twenty-year-old Walter Cronkite while consuming three liters of bier. I aspired to such knowledge and insight. I was also drunk, much like the previous evening, to the point that my alley toilet would beckon on my way home.

Because it was home. This city. This tourist trap of beauty. This honored, nearly sacred, place. Home in a way that every place in the States that I lived did not live up to. This hallowed ground held me.

Halfway to my upper destination, the trees opened to a glorious view of Altstadt, the Monchsberg, and the castle, with the Untersberg behind. I used to come to this spot to noodle through my early twenties emotions and, toward the end of my student time in Salzburg, to consider my options of staying or retreating, to parents and studies and eventually the love that distracted me from writing letters or returning, if even for a visit.

Engulfed in the intervening years, calcified in my reasons for what amounted to inaction, someone sat on the bench next to me. Assuming it was an Austrian Frau out for her midday climb through heaven, I excused myself and made to leave.

"You are so predictable, Greyling."

Shit. Shit. Shit, I mumbled to myself. I sat back down. "I wasn't aware of that," I said, looking beyond the Untersberg into the airspace above Germany. My bier-addled pique from yesterday returned.

Hansi touched my shoulder. "An observation is all. A welcome memory."

Damn. Damn. Damn, shambled through what coherence I could muster.

"I have frequently come here since my return to Salzburg a couple of years ago. Even with Andreas in my life I came here in my thoughts. During the rough times."

I turned toward him. "I imagined you had a perfect life. Medical school. Austria."

"The Sound of Music?" he laughed.

"The good bits at least, because you didn't escape to Vermont." I ventured a smile.

"Why do Americans think that Europeans want to move to the States?"

"Neo-colonial fascism?" I questioned with a grin.

"You went back to the pub. What a shame. Your memories are insulted by the rich ladies of Salzburg trampling your sanctuary. How cute."

"Don't be rude, Hansi, it's not like you."

"What do you know of me? I am not the Hansi of my youth. I am the Hans of too much power over other's lives and too much grief at too much loss."

"I am sorry."

"The embattled, embittered Greyling. The years have not been kind—it would seem."

Bird song disrupted my intended, inflammatory retort. "It's too beautiful here for more of that," I said.

"Perhaps another time, then," he replied.

"Is that what you want? To revisit our parting. If we are going to keep running into each other, maybe civility is a better companion." I stood and tweaked my ancient back.

He heard the vertebrae snap into alignment. "That didn't sound good," he said.

"Yeah. Well. Time has taken a toll."

"Sam, I'm a doctor. What's happened?"

"Hansi, or am I to call you Hans now that we have switched to grown-up first names?"

"What are you so angry about, mein Schatz?"

"Please don't call me that. Too much and too many have happened in between."

He stood and touched my shoulder again. I fought the urge to pull away.

"The fact is, Greyling, I live in this small town. For however many days you are here we will run into each other because I return to our favorite places, too. That will not change."

My shoulders slumped. "I am sorry."

"You still say that a lot, mein Schatz."

I turned toward him.

He pulled me into his chest. "If it makes your visit more comfortable, I will go visit Anna Marie in Vienna."

"Anna Marie?"

"My sister? She's first violin in the Wiener Staatsoper Orchestra. I'm due a visit. Andreas' younger brother is there, too."

"I remember her tagging along with us, never without her violin. She's that good, huh?"

"Her dream was the Philharmonic. She's content and still teaches some."

"I am sorry."

"Stop with that, will you. Why don't you come with me. We can stay with them. I can show you around modern Vienna, revisit Belvedere."

I pushed away to stand free.

"I see what you are doing, Hansi." I tweaked my head to one side.

"What am I doing, Samuel Scott Greyling?" He cocked his head in the same direction as mine. I felt mocked. He laughed loud enough to silence the birds for a moment. "You are always yourself."

I stepped back and looked at the view. "I am determined to get to the top of this mountain before sunset." I started past him to the path.

"And I have lunch with friends by Mirabell," he said.

"Did you come here looking for me, Hansi?"

"You have a habit of flattering yourself, Greyling."

"Enjoy Vienna," I said as I strode up the incline that quickly induced deeper breathing than I was used to. I didn't look back until I reached the top of a set of stone steps carved into the steeper path. Worn with a century of footfall, I stepped with caution. He had sat back on the bench and didn't move for several minutes. Then he stood, stretched his arms wide, and wandered slowly down toward the Steingasse entry. I watched him the entire way, an ancient longing wending through my aching body.

Bird song awakened me, as did an older couple on their way down the hill who pushed me aside without a simple 'excuse me.' The walking stick to my side was bad enough but the rudeness startled me.

"Haben noch einen schönen Tag," I raised my voice in defiance. Wishing them a good day was really meant for Hansi but he was out of range of my voice, and perhaps out of my life for good. The old man waved his arm dismissively.

I returned to my trek distractedly observing tree species, leaf differences, ferns and berry snags, and the ever-available bird song that I tapped into for motivation. Never good at ornithology, I didn't have a clue which birds were which. I chuckled at my ignorance, which returned me to my memory of the ranting student whose name I couldn't recall.

Since this trip was intended as a holiday and not a mountain adventure, I sat at the next bench. It faced into the managed forest. A common red deer hind wove in and out of the undergrowth. The thrill of seeing her nailed me to the spot hoping a faun or yearling would follow her into the iridescent woodland. No such luck.

I rested against the hardwood. The leaden air of midday warmed my lungs. The dapples of light moving over me warmed my skin. My lids fluttered near to the sleep that I hadn't had enough of to relieve another day of jetlag. I had to avoid the nap my body was nudging me toward. More hiking and a hearty goulash would reinvigorate me. I was about to stand to continue my last push toward the triumph of conquering this mighty hillock when another voice jostled for attention. It wasn't Hansi returning to rescue me, a thought I knew I would have to engage at some point soon.

In the local dialect a man said, "May I join you? Did you see the hind? Beautiful, nicht wahr."

"I am about to leave but yes, please. The bench is all yours."

"Your dialect? Styria, perhaps. Certainly not Tyrolian. Ah, perhaps Upper Austria. Not Viennese!" The startled hind darted up the hill abandoning any faun that probably wasn't there anyway. Smart animal. Running from invading humans.

I joined in his laughter because either he was mocking my accent, or he was fooled into near hysteria. Before I could build a lie, he continued.

"Do you come here often?" He turned to look up and down the path so he could drape his leg on the bench and nearly touch me.

Missing his meaning, I said, "Not enough. Apparently."

"Do you still go to that nighttime mash-up at Mirabell Gardens? That is too tiring and too full of tourists, especially pushy, demanding, uptight Americans who should be at their hotels with their wives and children."

Spoken like a knowing expert, I thought.

He continued, "There are some very hot men there. The effort is not worth the reward. What do you think?"

The pause was long enough for two or three hook-ups in a row.

"It is beautiful here," I diverted the conversation if not his intense gaze.

"My view is lovely," he whispered. "I live nearby. In Parsch."

Habsburg subtlety was not his strong suit.

"I am flattered. Perhaps another time," I lied twice.

He removed his leg from the bench and turned toward the forest, crossing his arms.

"Perhaps not." He gasped. "You aren't from here anyway and I am not known for one-night stands." He huffed and rose like Mary on a cloud of green trousers and sensible shoes. "Haben noch einen schönen Tag." Thrown back at me with similar abandon. He muttered down the hill.

Gathering myself from a scene that happens the world over, I marched the other direction until I reached the top of the hill. A little sad that there wasn't a retinue of encouraging throngs dispersing gold medals for my exertion, I turned downhill to find a lunch spot. I fancied a wheat bier so bee-lined to Zipfer in Altstadt. Buzzing through tourists in every direction I remembered how the buildup to the weekend meant more of them than earlier in the week. I needed to plan the weekend accordingly.

Zipfer Weissen bier has a flavor that rests on the tongue and slips down the throat with no bitterness or hoppy-ness as an aftertaste. From my first ever sip of it, wheat bier became my go-to brew when I am not downing scotches, bourbons, and other dark spirits.

I squeezed into a booth across from the bar. A liter of Weissen arrived three minutes later with a basket of bread. After my splurge last night, I settled for Bratwurst mit Senf und Kraut, figuring I could find a goulash another time. Easy fare served quickly. I was done and out of there in no time. I scuttled into the cathedral for a reminder of the beauty of middle Baroque architecture. The organist was practicing for the Mozart mass scheduled for 10:00 on Sunday. I would be avoiding that like the plague but sat contentedly as the effervescence of Weissen bier, with a hint of kraut, softly revisited my mouth. I giggled inappropriately as another tranche of tourists passed. Tourists bring their homegrown moralities and looks of disdain with them. I stuck my tongue out at their backsides while my impish gargoyle continued to giggle.

Without a plan for the day, I took the funicular up to the castle. I escaped the usual tourist routes to find secluded views of the city and countryside. My favorite vantage point was human free and I leaned against the battlements, encouraging memories.

Thomas jammed into my brain. I had tried to leave him back home, where he belonged and where I wanted him to stay.

Pain and longing wrapped around my heart, twisting and pulling in too many directions. When I looked south toward Hellbrunn, I remembered the fun and good times we shared for so many years. When I looked north toward Maria Plain, I was overcome by the sadness that still encased my memories of him. Someone along the way told me that loss and grief never go away. They become different with time. Knowing when 'different' happens had me stumped. I came back to Salzburg to find what might be different now. I begged the universe to let me heal. To let go of Thomas. To find a way to hold him close and view our life from afar. At the same time. I was failing both.

Hansi floated over the cathedral. His specter either invited me to a solution or mocked me for thinking a tourist trap city would offer a brief respite.

"Fuck you!" I screeched at the mirage.

I cursed Thomas for hanging around. I cursed Hansi for intruding. I cursed myself for holding one too close and the other too far away.

I lowered my head to rest on my crossed arms. Not one to cry in public, I held it together using my trained yogic breathing to calm my nerves and focus. Focus on what. Breathe into what. Breathe out from what. Confusion choked a cough out of me. My body expelled my frustration faster than my restful breathing ever could.

The course of the Salzach River pulled my attention into the mountains south of town. Maybe renting a car for an alpine drive would loosen these memories. It was too late today. The weekend would have tour busses clogging the valleys. The salt mines would be packed. Berchtesgaden requires a full day on its own. The Salztkammergut is best done with an overnight. Options for a single traveler are plentiful.

Being single at Augustiner's isn't so great.

I parked myself against the monastery inner garden wall at a table with one chair; the other one had been purloined for the loud and loutish party next to me. My liter stein and second Bratwurst mit Senf of the day beckoned, I looked up to see Hansi and three beshirted and beshorted Austrian men descend the staircase—steins and food trays in hand. One of them pointed in my direction, not because he knew me but because an empty four-seater was a couple of tables away. Hansi pulled him toward the outer wall seating. I was simultaneously relieved and perturbed.

I snarfed the brat and nursed my bier. I also nursed my annoyance, which grew with each gulp. To my credit, I bolted my ass to the chair and didn't move. I also girded my face so I wouldn't look in their direction, although I noted that Hansi sat with his back to me. I shifted my chair to further distance my gaze but was confronted with the group of tourists I had encountered in the cathedral, children included. Biergartens! Children. Pets. Annoying ex-boyfriends. All allowed.

Damn. There it was. Admitting that Hansi was an ex-boyfriend. I have had this rule that all my ex's stay friends. I have worked hard to make that true. A couple have fallen away but that was always their choice. I tried my best. They rejected me. Not my fault.

Today's conundrum is that I rejected Hansi, and for no good or decent reason, except living in different countries, growing up in different cultures, and being totally different people. I rejected him, not to his face as my exes deigned to, but by not replying to or writing letters for two years, until he mercifully stopped. Not sure who the mercy was for. He still thinks fondly of me. As I do him. He is my first ex.

I wanted to screech 'fuck you' again at the top of my lungs to chase these annoying patrons away so Hansi and I had the Biergarten to ourselves, so we could duke it out, verbally if not physically. I realized how arrogant that sounded as I plunked a few euros on the table to pay for a second liter. Judging on recent experience, I knew I should walk away, this time stopping in the pissoir, then out the main entrance so Hansi wouldn't see my retreat.

My relief was palpable when I saw the gaggle of gays retracing their steps up and presumably out of the monastery. My sigh must have been overly audible because the tourists turned and laughed what was probably for them an edifying snark. They didn't know why I sighed. They did know why I belched. We shared their second laugh at my expense. One of the kids playing in the bier-splattered gravel stuck his tongue out in my direction. I returned the favor. His mother, I assumed, reached down to turn his head away from me. I couldn't hear her tsk-tsk-tsk but saw it chatter over her lips. They prepared to leave. I chugged half a liter of bier.

It was too early for dinner even though in Salzburg most restaurants offer a blue-plate special as standard fare starting at 5:00 p.m., accommodating older locals and tired tourists. Younger, trendy Austrians dine at human hours. A few clubs may go late but those are few and far between. Students and adventurous others train to Munich or Vienna for weekend escapes.

I escaped Augustiner's to sit on a bench on the bike path along the Salzach, across from the evangelical church and this side of Mirabell Palace and gardens. It is a lovely view that encompasses the whole of the historic city and the modern sections off in the distance. Being below the berm the traffic noises recede. Occasional bicyclists, rollerbladers, and walkers intrude but at this time of day it is quiet enough.

"May I sit?" Hansi appeared.

"You're stalking me, Herr Wortmann."

He continued to stand.

"It's a fucking small town."

I could hear his smile.

"I thought you were going to Vienna."

I indicated the other end of the bench.

"I will leave on Sunday."

He waited for my nonexistent response.

"There's a party on Saturday. You could meet my friends. Please come."

Remembering Reinhardt's invitation, I said, "I have plans."

"Pinochle at the Center?" He referred to one of our student pastimes during the cold winter months.

I looked at him. He was half looking toward Kapuzinerberg while glancing in my direction.

Striking still. Greying but full headed. Three crow's feet each side. Nose northern European. Small ears. Ruddy cheeks. Slightly dimpled with a visible chin cleft. Straight-backed in his six feet. Still hot as fuck.

"I know what you are doing," I said.

"I wish you'd tell me. It is kindness to invite a guest to our city to a party where said guest might meet other people."

"This isn't about a party."

"Then what is it?"

I watched kayakers race north on the Salzach toward the River Inn, then on to the confluence with the Danube in the far distance. They looked kitted out for a journey. I wondered how they got back to their starting point. Or was their end point the beginning.

"Where would I start?" I ask.

"By talking. And walking. And not drinking so much alcohol that you piss on people's walls and in Steingasse alleyways."

"Should I be concerned that you are stalking me?" I tried to laugh this out of me but failed into a self-absorbed whine.

Hansi's laugh reminded me of the first day we encountered each other in the corner grocery store down the block from the Center and, it turned out, from his home that was next door to us. I walked in for some cookies that had become an obsession. His twenty-year old self was paying for cheese, eggs, and bier. As he turned to leave, he looked so deeply into me that I shuddered. Had I not had the cookies in one hand and money in the other I would have forgotten what I was doing. I watched him leave. Out on the sidewalk I froze. He was standing just past the Center having turned back to look in my direction. We considered each other until he walked into his family home. On wobbly legs I stopped at the end of the hedge to look after him. He stood inside the door looking out the window at me. Then he disappeared further into the house.

"Greyling," he stopped my memories, "talking with an old friend is not threatening. Unless. Well, unless you are afraid. Then I suppose it could feel that way."

Fuck. Fuck. Fuck. My brain cells contorted.

He said, "Why did you come back?"

The kayakers floated around the bend. I looked at the profile of my first love.

"Escape. Needing a new adventure, which for me is another way of saying escape."

What I needed in this moment was a single malt with a schnapps chaser, and a bier topper. In short, another wall-pissing drowning of my grief and fear. I knew this. I understood it in my core.

Hansi rested his hand on my shoulder, a long reach from the far end of the bench.

"What happened to you, mein Schatz?"

I shifted to settle my back against the bench. He raised his hand and scootched closer. His hand was firm against my bony shoulder. His gentle squeeze bolted through me.

"Please don't," I said. "I can't do this. Not with you."

"Wounds heal, Sam, if you let them."

I snorted. "You don't know my wounds or anything else. You with your movie life and movie looks and film noir storylines." My indignance slapped him in the face before it merged with the Salzach and raced toward the Danube.

"It would be rude of me to assume that I know your adventures. What I do know is the adventure we had for nearly a year. For me, it wasn't enough time. That's why I waited for you to come back or to tell me why you couldn't. I had adventures, too, Greyling. You seem so intent on your pain that you take no interest in me or how I came to this moment. I learned that waiting is the undercurrent of my life. Andreas knew that I had a deeper love than him. He accepted that and still had the capacity to love me very deeply. All I want is to tell you my adventure. Then to hear yours. Here. In Vienna. During drives to the valleys and lakes. Wherever we can talk. That is all. Then to say goodbye. Perhaps to understand." He turned away and sat ramrod straight. He pushed himself to standing. "I will leave the party details at your hotel. Come if you want. Or don't."

His alpine stride took him quickly away. I watched him walk under the footbridge. I leaned forward, elbows to knees. I glanced again to see him veer off up the slope of the berm.

"Fuck!" I shouted at the top of my lungs.

Hansi turned his head ever so slightly, enough for me to see a slight smile form then drop away.

What do I do with that, I thought.

I glanced to make certain he was out of sight. Standing, the tension pulsed in my muscles. I shook myself from head to toe, extending my legs to wiggle each foot. The stress in my neck loosened as I twisted and circled my head.

Why did he live in Salzburg. Innsbruck made more sense since he went to school there. Vienna even, because he was a driven, intense man. I didn't know what branch of medicine or anything else he was in.

My absentminded meander back to and through Altstadt lead me to Franziskanerkirche, the impressive gothic cathedral that embraces visitors in its darkness and cool flow of air. Not so great in winter but in summer it becomes a haven for the knowing who want to escape the humidity wafting up from the Mediterranean and the heat clouds stifling from the east. When the light is right the church glows with stained glass filtered rays of inspiration. On cloudy dismal days, the whole building bathes darkness into visitor's bones.

Franziskaner was my favorite church in Salzburg, and what pulled me here to ruminate on the conundrum I would like to blame on Hansi but I knew was my doing. For the first ten minutes I wandered the side aisles looking at but not registering the chapels and stations of the cross. I gazed into the ceiling marveling at the massive weight of that structure, made to look so light and airy.

I crawled into a pew and slid along until I had the right vantage to see as much of the beauty as I could, enough back from the center so beams of light wouldn't hit me. Hiding from inspiration.

Dealing with Thomas' death had been a slow, torturous path that led nowhere. I tapped into my grief easily because it rested between my third and fourth layers of skin, barely deep enough to conceal but always easy to access. After three plus years I should be letting go. I could move on. Others who have lost husbands moved on, I always thought too soon but I am not them.

Counselling didn't help yet I had to admit that I could be in worse shape or dead from my impulses. I never really went there but the urges were at times palpable and needed wrangling from time to time.

Sitting engulfed in magnificence I relaxed into my breathing practice. I took up one of my mantras about dying and life. Breathe in living. Breathe out dying. Ying. Yang. Not opposites. Not the same.

The clatter of a dry dust mop against the pews woke me from my meditation.

"Zehn Minuten bis zum Feierabend," said the young man. "Zehn Minuten, bitte."

"Ja, richtig," I stuttered. "Genau," I replied.

He winked.

I blushed.

I smiled approval and nodded to the crucifix with the nearly naked Jesus suspended in an early version of erotic torture, assuming that was anywhere near historical, which I always thought it wasn't, but who am I.

As I wandered out to the subsiding bustle of Altstadt, the young man held the small door within the huge wooden doors open for me. Being the last visitor of his day, presumably— because who knows who a horny sacristan might have hidden away in some nook or cranny of his gothic office, he winked again, "Auf wiedersehen bis zum nachsten mal."

I kept my reply to the simple, "Wiedersehen." No hint that if he didn't have a gentleman in his sacristy, he could invite me back through the door. I thought it but revealed nothing. Thomas was rising through my flesh.

I sat on the steps for a few minutes. Getting Thomas to take a healthy seat further away from me was proving difficult. I pictured him back home in his easy chair. Images of him dying in that same chair and me finding him when I bull rushed into the house with groceries and that damn dog of his. I walked right passed him in his death scene telling him about running into Lyndie at the store and all the drama in her life. I put groceries away. Watered the dog. Peed. Made a phone call to Gary then sat in the kitchen with a cool, local brew wondering about my life and when Thomas was going to die or not.

It wasn't all that long before I checked on him. Stone cold. Breathless. Body decaying as I indulged my own need for a break, if ever so brief.

The doctors had said he could go in the next week or so. He didn't want tubes and medical staff and emergencies and poking and prodding. He chose to die at home. While it was too soon, it was also time. After eighteen months of surgeries and suffering he'd had enough.

Sitting on these steps in Salzburg, Austria I finally admitted that I had had enough of him dying too.

Some form of exhaustion got me through the planning and the funeral and the family visiting and our friends grieving. Six months later I was in therapy because none of my friends gathered my grief in their arms and squeezed me until I felt whole again. They were nice. They were respectful. They were encouraging. Perhaps I had demanded too much of them. The loneliness of death permeated my every thought. My reaching out got nothing in return.

That's why I returned to Salzburg after all these years. It was my womb. It was solace. It was the one place on the planet where I felt whole.

It may have been me, but I never felt whole with Thomas. I loved him beyond words. I cherished him even when we fought like rutting animals. Being complete? Not once. Contentment, yes indeed. Happiness? Thoroughly. But the 'us' of the relationship never fully gelled. We talked of us. We used the language of us. It never seeped into my bones. I don't think it did with him, either. Nor, I think, did we think it could.

Except that I knew it could because I had embraced 'us' with Hansi.

That reality smacked me in the face, sitting on the steps of my favorite church. The agony of it blurred my vision. The tourists and shop owners going home at the end of the day smudged my awareness like a modernist painting. The smear of humanity neither inviting nor repelling. Red. Blue. Green. Grey. Yellow. Purple. Smeared to black.

I was spent. Thomas and Hansi caught up with me in one swoosh of modernity.

To not be overcome, I trudged to my hotel. A nap before dinner was welcome.

Passing by the front desk, the concierge motioned to me. "Hand delivered, Herr Greyling."

He handed me two envelopes of identical stationery.

"Danke sehr." I turned toward the lift.

"Bitte sehr. Do you need a dinner reservation, Herr Greyling?"

"I'll phone down in a minute."

I sat in the brocade covered side chair that angled toward the window with the postcard view. Both envelopes in my hand. Each an answer to my conundrum. Each a way in or a way out. Breathe in. Breathe out. I couldn't meditate their content into my brain. I contemplated one other option, which was to leave all together. Abandon Salzburg. Go to Venice or Paris or Amsterdam or London or home. Accept that even this story book city held no story or adventure for me now.

The weight of two small envelopes grew too heavy. I placed them on the windowsill to open later. I lay on the bed to rest my eyes, not bothering to remove shoes or shirt. I nestled my head into the pillow heaving a sigh of relaxation.

I awoke when my muscles spasmed. The light was soft and dreamy. I looked at the bedside clock. I had only dozed for twenty minutes.

Time to arrange dinner.

"The concierge has not arrived yet today, Herr Greyling. May I assist?"

"He said he'd help with a dinner reservation."

"I can do that, sir. Do you have a preferred restaurant for this evening? We can confirm your seating once they open at 11:00."

I glanced at the clock again.

"It's 6:20. Surely, they can take a single person now?"

"Now, sir? Breakfast is included in your room rate."

"What time is it?"

"Are you alright, Herr Greyling? It's 6:20 a.m."

"I'll call back." I hung up the phone.

The morning light was growing, shining off Hohensalzburg onto the windowsill and the two envelopes I had ignored the night before.

Three

Back in my room after breakfast, I stood at the door surveying my domain. Housekeeping had done their thing. Five hundred square feet of my kingdom cleaned and tidied. This kind of service is why I never liked those internet apartment renting options. When I travel, I want to feel that I am on vacation, not having to clean and tidy.

I glanced to the windowsill. No envelopes awaiting my perusal. I spied them on the bedside table laid side by side aligned to the edge of the gold embossed trim. First class service, indeed.

After brushing my teeth and changing shirts and footwear to fit the weather, I sat on the bed considering what to do. With what had become my typical approach to life after Thomas' death, I decided to wait until later in the day, contemplating the option of tossing both, unopened, into the waste basket that beckoned, gape-mouthed next to the nightstand. Haste would not make waste—at the moment.

Slipping my phone out of my trousers I dialed the international number for my airline. I paced around the bed stopping to glance at the inviting view. I sat in the side chair. My leg crossed and my foot running a marathon, I listened to the electronic repeated message with background electronic noises impersonating music, counting the dollars sweeping out of my bank account with each encouragement to please wait someone will be with you shortly.

"$500 to change my flight?" I contained my shout as best I could. "What if I wait a day or two does that go down?"

Negotiating with functionaries following scripted rules never gets a satisfactory result. Requesting the manager when this avenue of escape was my doing wouldn't get any result. I dropped the idea for now, telling myself I could revisit it tomorrow or the next day.

Perturbed with myself I peed, grabbed what I thought I needed for wandering a city that was slowly closing in on me, and trundled out the door. I was going to avoid any place that was familiar and memory inducing, which meant avoiding Hansi at all costs.

The concierge was sad to inform me that most day trips by coach had already left town. He offered to book one for tomorrow. Perhaps I could rent a bicycle. That intrigued me but I also knew it was a strain that would set me back a day or two afterwards. I wasn't worried about getting to a destination or an imagined half-way point. It was the return that would kill me.

What I knew Hansi wouldn't do was local museums.

The concierge talked me into a seven-day, all-venue ticket that would get me passed the queues via the fast lane if the venue had a fast lane. It would work on the funicular and the lift to the modern art museum, the former casino on Monchsberg. It would also give him a hefty kickback.

I didn't come to Salzburg to be a tourist. I came to meld into my memories. Yet, here I was, buying into the concept with the sole purpose of avoiding Hansi.

My first stop was the Konditorei where I'd breakfasted the day before. I needed another shot of caffeine to endure the hordes.

Thoroughly buzzed, I ventured to the Salzburg Museum to waste a couple of hours looking at what I already knew or had seen before. An attendant asked if I wanted to join a tour that was forming and would begin in five minutes. I thanked him. As I turned toward the exit he nodded in a knowing way. I smiled politely with no hint of interest.

I scuttled across Domplatz to its dramatic sculptural centerpiece. I crawled into the shady side and scrunched into a comfortable position on a narrow shelf of marble to watch the world go by. It wasn't long before two Polizei ventured my way to admonish me in demanding voices to vacate or be arrested for damaging historic artifacts. So much for reliving that memory of avoiding my early twenties' depression in the middle of winter when the Polizei couldn't be bothered to shoo me away.

Nearing midday and heating up because there was no air movement to speak of, I chanced the walk across the river to the Zwelgelgarten on the Bastion that provided sheltered relief with huge lindens protecting the stone dwarf sculptures from sun and air pollution. On the way I picked up a charcuterie, cheese, and pickle sandwich with a bier to go for a picnic on the grass. When I got there the 'stay off the grass' sign more than annoyed me but I sat on the edge of it anyway hoping no more cops would disrupt my avoidance scheme.

After dining, I lay back on the cool turf. The slight dampness soaked in, chilling me to a comfortable degree. I floated over myself in an imagined out of body moment.

Deal with the mess, flounced from my wispy self into my corporeal self. Damn. Damn. Damn, flitted back and forth in a nauseating bifurcated dance.

I sat up and looked around at the dwarves—stone cold in their disinterested stares.

"Guys," I said out loud not caring if others were witness to my craziness, "help me out here. Give me a clue. What the fuck am I to do?"

The remainder of the ambient temperature bier coursed neutrally through my gullet and gut.

"Appropriate reply, guys, thanks."

I lowered my head to my knees. A tail end of jetlag tugged at my energy. Curling up on the grass for a nap would have done a world of good. My trash pile would have made me look indigent. I surmised. I stood to get blood flow into my limbs and to loosen my brain for the last push to sanity.

I meandered from dwarf to dwarf recalling how this small park was one of my favorites because of its seclusion. It was fortress-stoned-dwarf in those days. Easily accessed and providing a refuge from group activities, required study prep, and too much Austrian cultural exposure. It was another place of escape.

The pattern was becoming comically obvious.

The faces of the dwarves turned from mocking to sympathetic, offering a kind self-indulgence. I smiled as I touched each one on the head and took a few selfies with my new best friends.

The day became more peaceful. Letting go of the stress softened my gait. Abandoning my frown unburdened me. I walked east listening to the music coming from practice rooms. A viola repeated phrases of a Mozart sonata working toward perfection. An oboe wafted delicately through a passageway. I paused for a voice with piano to finish an aria. Floating in the sublime is freeing. Holding sublimity is a treat. I held it close until I found myself on the Steingasse outside the bar from the other night.

What the heck. I let the peacefulness waft away as I entered a Saturday afternoon gathering of gay men and a few women.

The bartender waved and lifted the bottle of single malt I had half-drained before Rheinhardt politely escorted me to my hotel. I nodded agreement and made my way to the same stool at the far end of the bar. It was indulgent to think they had reserved this perch for me. The tumbler with lovely golden relaxation and a bowl of mixed nuts waited patiently.

"Prost," I toasted the bartender and a few men looking at me lustfully in the mirror. I enthroned on the stool and slouched against the wall. One drink, I promised, cross my heart, which I didn't physically do because I wasn't sure if the gesture was culturally specific to Anglo-Saxon-Americans and I didn't want to confuse it with the sign of the cross, which is more understood in this nominally Roman Catholic 'Rome of the North'.

The journey from the sublime to alcoholic warmth slithering down my throat was welcome. The heights of the arts can be balanced with the release of a relaxing tipple—or two.

"Herr Greyling, nice to see you again," Rheinhardt whispered in my ear as he leaned around me.

"Hello, young man," I said, welcoming the touching. "Don't you work tonight?"

"Oh Ja. Until closing. Saturday. Big night. Sticking with bier until the party. You are coming to the party, yes?"

"Shouldn't you be at the restaurant?" I got all parental and annoying.

"Vatti gave me permission to avoid set up and prep—only for today, he said."

"I will visit you again there soon." I said, washing a few nuts down with my drink.

"I better see you before then, Herr Greyling. Family names are so boring. Remind me your human name?"

"Sam," I said with a smile.

"Sam, pleased to know you," he kissed me square on the lips. The wet of his kiss excited me. A jolt in my loins startled me. I pulled back.

"That was rude of me," he blushed.

"Unexpected is all," I smiled to relieve whatever tension was between us.

"Promise me you will be there," he said.

I waited a few seconds to reply.

"I will see how I feel at the time," was my escape route.

He looked at his oversized, copper-colored watch, "Oh, I must go. I will have to run."

He kissed me again, "I'll see you tonight, Sam!"

He breezed through the room pecking cheeks and touching faces. He left a swirl of smiles until he was gone. A sweet man making others happy if only for a peck and a poke.

I took Reinhardt's departure as a hint. I downed my drink, popped a few more nuts into my gob, tossed a few too many euros onto the bar, and waved goodbye to the bartender.

"So soon?" he shouted through the din.

'Yes', I mouthed and waved again.

The cool air and smells of the Steingasse were pleasing and invigorating. It was a good day, odd at times, but satisfying and relaxing.

Back in the room, intending to read the notes that vexed me, there was a metal box of Mozartkugeln. The blue box. Blue for the original recipe of pistachio, marzipan, and dark chocolate. Delicious in memory. Exquisite to taste.

An accompanying enveloped note in the concierge's hand read, "Forever. –Anonymous"

Weird. Fucking weird.

And—what?

First off, this is an unwelcome distraction whatever it turns out to be. If it is a joke, then it is quite simply a sick one. Maybe. Damn. Damn. Damn.

Second, do I spend time in *that* distraction or deal with the immediate one of two invitations to two parties. Fuck. Fuck. Fuck.

The concierge picked up on the first ring. Another thing I like about this class of hotel is the quality of service that puts guests first over staff. Civilized.

"Yes, Herr Greyling, how may I assist?"

"These Mozartkugeln. Who. When. How." Sentences abandoned me.

"Yes, sir. They appeared in a smart unmarked shopping bag delivered by a driver in a Mercedes. A note in the bag requested that I write the card you received."

"Did you add the 'anonymous' signature?"

"Part of the instructions, Herr Greyling."

"Do you have the instructions?"

"No, sir. However, they did arrive right after you left this morning."

"I see," I said, no wiser than five minutes ago. "Thank you. Oh, sorry, can you find a medium-priced restaurant for dinner. 8:00 or 8:30?"

"Do you wish a location in Altstadt or may I select one that I know you will enjoy."

"Get me one that only locals go to but not in Nonntal."

Dining sorted out.

I went with my gut about the gift. Hansi being circumspect. Who else could it be. Reinhardt didn't know me well enough to order delivery. The concierge or hotel staff wouldn't do that either, they'd default to a hotel something or other. A wink from a sacristan wouldn't evolve into a gift that was too expensive for his income. I was left with Hansi.

Or. Perhaps one of my U.S. friends might call in a delivery. Nah, they wouldn't stay anonymous. They'd want credit for creativity and timing, which for them most probably meant a drunken night of inspiration. Also, a caper of this quality was beyond them, especially if booze was involved. Further, to put a fine point on dismissing this option, I hadn't told my friends I was vacationing in Austria. I had absconded to avoid their questions and pique as part of my post-Thomas avoidance. I accepted that it was Hansi intruding again.

I showered then wrapped myself in the logo'ed, Egyptian cotton robe for a micro nap. When I awoke twenty-five minutes later, I heard the swoosh of something being shoved under the door. Another envelope. The economy of this country must run on envelopes flying all over the place. I avoided it to break into the minibar for a one finger tipple before dressing.

Resting in the window chair, single malt in hand, I marveled at how Hohensalzburg was built stone on stone on the top of a hill in the middle of a city. Back lit by the evening light it radiated power and presence, towering over the river valley that would not have been tamed at the time. It is said that the castle had never been breached, with many stories, hilarious and serious, about how the besieged survived.

A second envelope slipped into my castle keep. Besieged by mail. Hilarious and likely serious.

I traipsed to the door, scooped up the envelopes, and floated in mock seriousness back to bed, arranging the pillows for sitting comfortably with scotch in hand.

First envelope. Hotel stationery. The concierge had secured a table. A car would be waiting because it is a twenty-minute drive away. Promising. He didn't mention the restaurant so I couldn't research it online. A Saturday night adventure. I can do that. Trusting another person to get it right. Dubious.

Second envelope. Hotel stationery again. Obvious handwriting. I tossed it across the bed unopened. Hansi effusing his excitement to see me. Not sure why I was surprised, I slapped my face with both hands. "Lighten up, Greyling," I said out loud. I silenced myself with a swig of booze, intrigued that I never refer to my inner self as Greyling preferring effervescent condemnations of the cursing type.

If I go to his party, should I take the blue tin of chocolate goodness as a hostess gift or should I mention it at all or if I mention it, how do I mention it. It would be rude not to, but it would also be fun to pretend I never got such a lovely gift. Scotch sloshed into my sinuses when I snorted my laugh. The burn elicited another snort. Repeat and enjoy.

Third envelope. I twirled it between my fingers. Held it up to the light of the small, elegant, crystal chandelier centered in the room. No clues which one I held. Turned out to be Reinhardt's. Clipped cursive scrunched into the upper part of the card. If I take my time at dinner I can arrive late, then leave early. A courtesy call. Like social gatherings in Maria Theresa's Austria, I can treat it like a salon. Pay my respects to the host. Compliment the quality of the gathering. One drink. One canape. Out the door. Home by 11:30. In bed an hour later because of another single malt in the minibar.

I called the concierge to confirm his arrangements and the timing of the car.

Dressed in a grey, American cut suit with conservative striped tie and pocket square with black belt and shoes, I was driven miles out of Salzburg, approaching the base of the Untersberg. I somewhat knew this area, from decades before trekking around small villages, up and over hillocks, and along rivers and streams. That familiarity didn't help this evening.

We stopped in front of a modern, exquisitely designed, two-storied, wood stone building that melded into the surrounding forest. Ground-focused exterior lighting defined a gentle visual footprint if not a healthy carbon one. In the summer afterglow, darkened by the mountain behind, the restaurant shimmered in its natural foliage. The image evoked an elfin glen.

Emerging from the car, I attempted to pay the driver. I added to the gratuity that she said was already included. Naturally it would appear on my bill at departure.

The gush of flowing water pulled me up the path. A doorman stepped out of somewhere. A hostess greeted me in perfect English.

"We have a much sought-after table for you, Herr Greyling," she said with a Rococo smile, cheeks sensually rouged, lips matted a Moroccan red, and hair held back by a floral headband with real flowers. Looks of a pageant formal

Olympian. If I were straight, my non-Grecian body would be wilting with desire.

The restaurant, and therefore my seat, was cantilevered over the rushing torrents of the River Weissbach. I had once walked the path that the construction of this gorgeous place must have obliterated. Mesmerized, I was excited for the menu.

That convenience for ordering did not arrive.

What did arrive was a two-finger American bourbon neat.

The perplexion on my face brought the maître d' running.

"Herr Greyling, may I assist?"

Sentences left my brain for the second time today.

"Who? What? Confused?"

"Herr Greyling, you will be dining Prix Fixe this evening. We can provide a printed description of each course if you wish. We were assured you were experienced in Michelin dining."

"Ah. Who?"

"Herr Stohl placed your reservation."

"Stohl?"

"The concierge at your hotel. Georg Stohl."

"Ah."

"Would you prefer to enjoy your bourbon, or would you like us to begin with your first course and pairing?"

"Ah?" I had to get a grip. The rush of the river joined my addled brain. "Fifteen minutes. Then begin. Slowly please. I wish to savor your cuisine."

I also wished to figure out what the fuck was going on. Hansi has a lot to explain. That was a commitment to go to his party. I should be able to register my anger in five sentences then depart for Rheinhardt's party. Conundrum defused.

Sweet bourbon lolled on my tongue. The oaks and honeys merged into Appalachian malted rye. Its sourness warmed its way down. Memories of tasting rooms filled with options of the best of the best, shared with Thomas and other friends. I glanced out the window to unobtrusively wallow in sadness for a few seconds. For me, the darker the bourbon the better. The dark brew withered emotional inhibitions. Memories raced through me.

I dammed that flow with newer thoughts of Hansi. I knew he wanted closure regarding my missteps of years before. I supposed that I did, too. However, this dramatic show was theater of the absurd. While grateful, it was too much. It would go down in history as an overstatement of expectations. It was also not like him to be this showy. A little over the top at times but he had never done something like this. Then again, intervening years could do anything to a man. Prime example is the one enjoying a stupendous meal.

The Prix Fixe was eleven courses with paired wines and spirits. The village-shot venison microdallions marinated in forty-year single malt was exactly what the name said. According to the maître d' the hapless hind meandered into the wrong village at the wrong time of the year heading for the wrong herb and vegetable gardens. Apparently, a deer causing—or with the potential to cause—harm can be humanely eliminated from the breeding stock of its species. No humans or property were damaged in the one-way shoot-out. With the restaurant and gardens straddling the borders of Germany and Austria I was curious which laws of the land applied. I would never know because more courses excited my palate.

Eleven courses of food paired with thirteen wines and spirits—followed by one more to fortify me against what was to come—took over two hours. A delightful time I longed to share with one or a few others.

The bill did not arrive, yet the hostess encouraged me out the door. Whoever planned this had a generous streak and would need to be thanked profusely once I learned who it was. I was starting to doubt it was Hansi as the same driver eased me into the back seat and helped with the safety belt.

"Hotel, bitte," I said.

"I am instructed to take you elsewhere," she said glancing at my inquisitive brow furrow.

My fumbling hand went awry and into my suitcoat pocket. The opened party note from Rheinhardt was there. I turned my brain over three or four times trying to recall the address that might not have registered at all or was chased out by the second note.

Nestled inside the flap of Rheinhardt's envelope was the unopened invitation.

I brandished both to the driver. "I am not sure which destination I require," I said, my s's and r's evidence of thirteen pairings.

"I want to change clothes. You can wait outside since someone else seems to have bribed you for the evening."

She nodded her head in agreement.

"I'm not a prisoner in this charade. Or am I?" I looked for a response. She hadn't heard me as she rounded the front of the car to her door.

Twenty minutes later I was gliding through the lobby, lifts in sight.

"Herr Greyling, you are back sooner than expected," said the concierge.

"You are working late, Herr Georg Stohl."

"Saturday night. Opera. Theater. Guests with needs."

I must work on my grammar. "Who? When? How?"

"Anonymous," he smiled.

"Is he though?"

He tilted his smile further toward his epauletted shoulder.

"Weissbach is quite indulgent, nicht wahr?"

"Quite."

In my room I removed the suit and tie, dropping them in the window chair for all the mighty royals and dignitaries in the Hohensalzburg cemetery to see.

I changed into casual wear and splashed water on my face and neck. I added a whisper of cologne because showering would be rude to the driver. Then again, I'm not paying for the driver. Still, it was 11:00 pm. I attempted to talk myself into staying in but the glow of booze, the stimulating wash, and the embarrassment of wearing cologne to watch Austrian television was too much.

I felt powerless climbing back into the car. I inadvertently left the invitations in the suitcoat.

"Drive on, driver!"

I could have walked.

The north end of Getreidegasse was five minutes from the hotel. By car less than two. At this hour, no delivery vans and no pedestrians meant fast transport across Altstadt. She pulled up a few doors down.

"Wait," I said, "this can't be right."

"You'd be wrong about that, Herr Greyling. I'll ring then help you up the stairs. I'm to return at 2:00 a.m. So you know."

"I'll walk, thanks."

"You'll be wrong about that, too, Herr Greyling."

"What the fuck is going on? Do you know?"

"I think you are about to find out, sir."

The buzzer buzzed. The door opened. The heat and smell of bodies escaped. The sounds of music and laughter echoed. She didn't help me up the stairs. She drove away.

I leaned into the entry. At the top of the stairs all I could see was a pair of legs in a pair of white trousers, sandals on naked feet.

"Wilkommen," shouted above the din.

I stepped tentatively into the short hallway and slammed the door behind.

"What the fuck is this and who the fuck are you?"

Four

Rheinhardt gathered me in his arms. He kissed me full on the lips.

"You are late, Sam!" he said.

"Your restaurant can't be closed this early on a Saturday," I replied through two or three more kisses.

"Dad got tired of me moaning so he kicked me out. I must go in early tomorrow to do all the cleaning and prep. The price of a good time."

"A good time, indeed," I hazarded.

"There's someone I want you to meet," he said, his arm contorted around my neck in the narrow hallway. "He's holding court. You'll love him. Don't say you won't. You are a lover. I know these things."

Our symbiod-self pushed into the living room and through a concentrated gaggle of gays. Rheinhardt nearly said what I was sure he was thinking as he pointed to the royal gag ensconced in a large wing-backed chair with a tartan woolen throw across his lap. Ta dah! I nudged him in the ribs to make him release my neck and breathing apparatus.

I recognized the queen gag as she herself raised up, allowing the tartan to drop to the floor, throwing his arms wide with splashes of his cocktail landing on a young man's face.

"Samuel Greyling," Gunther Drecker shouted. "Who ever thought this day would arrive."

Two minced steps. I was engulfed with his overly large hug, kisses to the neck, booze dribbling down my party frock, and a gut he didn't have all those years ago pushing me away. It was awkward on too many levels.

"Gunther," I amused, "lovely to see you again. You haven't changed at all."

"Still a liar," he said to the crowd of worshippers who laughed heartily while whispering and nodding to each other.

"When did I lie to you," I said.

"Every time we were together, Liebchen." He held me at arm's length. "More handsome than the day you abandoned us."

"Too, too kind, Gunther. What has your court been discussing? I recall you were fond of discussions, as long as we discussed you." The assembled laughed.

Gunther's hand stroked my back then fell away. My cringe relaxed. Rheinhardt arrived with a four-finger scotch. I sucked at least one of those fingers to the bone.

Gunnar—and I may have been the only person allowed to call him that—returned to his throne. The wet-faced young one arranged the throw on his lap just so before his hands were slapped away.

"Did you enjoy Weissbach?" he said. One eyebrow twittered in either glee or regret.

"I would love to thank my host for their generosity. Is he here do you think, Gunnar?"

He twisted his wrist to rest his hand on the side of his face, his little finger stroking the edge of his mouth.

"I wouldn't know," he glared across the other side of the room. "Perhaps we should ask everyone." He changed to German, "Requesting silence!" He looked back at me. "How is your German these days, Samuel, do you want me to translate or slow down for you to catch up?"

I charmed with my smile.

"No need, darling." I ventured across the void to lean down to kiss him on the cheek intending a French three-way peck. He turned enough toward me that our lips met.

He whispered, "Luscious as always, my dear."

"Thank you for the unexpected and sumptuous evening, Gunnar. It would have only been better had you been there."

"Liar," still whispering but with a hint of humor.

"You could have phoned when you knew I was in town," I said pulling back. His hand shot out to hold me closer in an uncomfortable position. I steadied myself on one of the wings of the chair as much for stability as to avoid scotch in his hair.

"Where's the fun in that when one can afford the theater," he released me before I collapsed onto his lap. "Now that you know where I am, perhaps we can dine one evening, you and me. I know another Michelin option requiring a drive to Vienna or a little further to Venice. I can schedule my driver with short notice." He tweaked his head so slightly that I doubted anyone else noticed.

"I'll have my people contact your people."

Gunther smiled.

"Wednesday isn't good for me." He reached out and grabbed the hand of his toy then leaned down to lick the dried cocktail from his face before going in for the French option.

I backed into Rheinhardt who slunk his arm around my neck again.

"Isn't he delightful?" He wagged a finger from his glass toward Gunther.

"He can be," I said extracting myself to dash into the dining room calculating when and how to depart. I wondered if there was still time to get to Hansi's party but realized I didn't have that invitation with me. Damn. Damn. Damn. I thought it rude to politely ask others if they knew where it was. I set my drink on the table sans coaster. Stain away, I chuckled to myself.

"Leaving so soon?"

Speak of the Krampus and one appears.

"Hello," I said more congenially than I was thinking, given the number of times I had been beaten with birch branches during the December of my student year. Hansi laughed uproariously the first time it happened but defended me the other times. Neither of us could figure out why I was a target for blood-inducing beatings until we discovered the guy playing the

Krampus in Maxglan and Neutor was a closet case seeking some sort of nasty revenge for something he perceived I must be doing or not doing.

"Do you have a cramp? Or is your distorted face because you are now reacquainted with him?"

"Neither. I recalled you saving me from the Krampus."

Quick chuckle.

"That asshole died of AIDS."

"That's not good."

"We know he infected at least three guys from his closet so there's that moral dilemma."

"Painful times for everyone," I touched his lower arm. "What happened to your party?"

He picked up my single malt and handed it back.

"This is my party! Didn't you read my invitation?"

"The way he—I assumed this was his house."

"This meagre thing in the middle of the tourist part of town? He has property and a large contemporary mansion just out of town. Made a fortune in travel and tourism. You likely used his websites and searches to book your return to the land he likes to reign over."

I must have looked askance or confused.

"Your new buddy, Rheinhardt, invited him. Unbeknownst to me. He arrived in his car before the driver went to whisk you away. I assumed you'd walk over. Oh well, Gunther rides again."

"Hold on. I thought you lived on Neutorstrasse, next to the Center."

"I inherited that from Dad. I rent it because I was living in Lucerne. You'd know this if you would take the time to talk to me. Do you think I'd invite Gunther into my home? I'd like to toss his ass out on the street."

I pulled a chair out from the table and plopped into it. He sat next to me.

"Greyling, I am about to kick everyone out anyway. The cops will be called soon if I don't. Stay behind. I'll fill you in."

I scratched my furrowed brow.

"One hour," he said.

"I've had too much to drink."

"Unlike you," he aimed for funny, I think.

"Seriously? Now? You have guests to disappoint." I stood to leave.

I turned back. "Are there any brunch places in this town?"

"I'll see if I can get us a table up at the Schloss," he said.

"Less than an hour ago I finished an eleven-course meal with thirteen pairings. Simple is better I think."

He chewed his lip.

"Hansi, you don't need to impress me." I touched his arm again. He placed his hand on mine. "There's never been a competition. Be gentle with the Holy Roman Emperor in there."

"He'll be angry if you don't say auf wiedersehen."

"The consequences of choices," I touched his shoulder, holding him back from a kiss or a hug. "11:00 at my hotel?"

"With bells on."

"No. One queen is more than enough."

I left into the warm summer air that felt chilly after the party heat.

Damn, I thought. Should have said good night to Rheinhardt.

Five

"Herr Greyling? Herr Greyling, this is the manager."

Pounding on my door.

"Shit. Shit. Shit."

I had unplugged the phone.

"One moment," I croaked. Not loud enough because the hotel manager stood at the corner of the short hallway a few steps inside my room.

"Herr Greyling, is everything all right?

"Clearly not or I'd be in the lobby."

"You have a guest in the lobby who is most concerned. What am I to tell him?"

"Time?"

"Nearly midday, sir."

"Who's in the lobby?"

"Herr Wortmann. He indicated you were brunching with him at 11:00 a.m. Your phone." He pointed either with his finger or his tone.

"I'll plug it in. My bad."

"Your guest?"

"Twenty minutes. Can you get a coffee sent up asap?"

He strode to the phone and did the plugging for me. He spoke to the restaurant stuttering the room number followed by, "Double-shot Café Americano. Black. Schnell, bitte."

"Please never unplug the phone. For your security. I am sure you understand, Herr Greyling." He closed the door behind him.

Hansi looked at his watch as I stepped out of the lift.

"You're paying, Herr Greyling," he said.

"I can't tell you how sorry I am. You know I'm never late for anything."

"No, I don't know, and you are today," he cuffed me on the shoulder.

"Where to?"

"I got a table at the Schloss."

"Hansi!"

"You're buying, so cheer up."

Bank accounts be damned.

The conductor on the funicular droned his bored overview of Salzburg history and one funny story about how a cow was touted around the battlements to prove the besieged castle's inhabitants had ample food to survive. An American tourist said, "One cow?" The conductor moaned his repartee, "They kept painting it different colors." He looked annoyed that no one had figured it out or maybe read it on the internet. I gave him a ten-euro tip and thanked him for his deadpan service. I wondered how many castles around Europe told the same story.

The afternoon view toward the Untersberg was glorious as ever. Hansi pulled the maître d' aside explaining the situation.

Our freshly cleared and reset table practically hung over the valley. Both chairs faced the view. We didn't see what the kerfuffle was behind us, but I suspected it was the guests who requested this table. It was going to be a tip-heavy brunch and a champagne apology moment.

Before the waiter could open his mouth, I said, "Please send a bottle of champagne to—"

"I already did that." Hansi waved the waiter away. "I also said they could order an appetizer on you. Oh, and a dessert if they want one."

"Just tell 'em to send me their entire bill while you're at it," I said.

"I thought that might be overdoing it." He grinned as he snapped my serviette onto my lap.

"Comme ci, comme ça," I shook my head to the snap of his serviette.

A bottle of champagne arrived with tall, modern crystal flutes.

"Are you ordering the entire meal, or do I get a chance, since I am paying for four?" I tried to be annoyed but that dissolved.

Brunch was continental. Not as in croissants and coffee in Paris, or scones and tea in London, but as in plates loaded with delights from many countries of Europe. A feast for the eyes and the taste buds. We ended with black Russians for a jolt of energy after a sumptuous meal. The maître d' billed our meal, and that of the displaced but now happy, affianced couple, to my hotel. Civility reigns in distant lands.

Rather than join the descending queue for the funicular we walked down the steep service road then cut through Nonntal around the Monchsberg to Lake Leopoldskron. We found a lakeside bench far enough away from tourists re-enacting scenes from *that* film. Their shouting and laughter, and the car horns demanding they move, still intruded but the visual of the Schloss glistening on the breeze-swept lake enchanted, as it does.

"Thank you," I said, leaning back, weaving my hands behind my head.

"You paid."

"Now you owe me," I turned my head enough to see him side-looking at me, too.

"Greyling, we don't owe each other anything."

"I mean—you are taking me to dinner one of these nights!"

"Ja. Naturlich." He lowered his head and looked away.

"Hansi, let's not get serious today. Brunch was lovely. I'm caught up on your family. You're caught up on mine. Leave it at that." I touched his shoulder. "For now."

"Do you realize—"

"I realize. I don't understand."

"What are you talking about?"

I removed my hand.

"I realize you loved me for years after I left. I don't understand why you would hold onto that for so long."

"What I was going to say before your rudeness, which you have a much larger capacity for than you used to, was that this is the day all those centuries ago, centuries might I inform you that I loved Andreas with all my heart, that you left and flew home."

"But, Hansi, am I right? Love and loss?"

"You do want to get into this."

"Yes. No. Not now. Hans, I don't know."

"Kind of like that day. Depart. Stay. Don't know," he said.

"I couldn't stay. I was on a student visa. I didn't have work. Back then I wouldn't get a work visa unless I found a job that an Austrian couldn't do. No options, Hansi. You knew that."

"Dad said he'd come up with something. They were as disappointed as I was."

"Did they figure it out."

"They knew I was happy."

"Would he have lied to create an import job that only an American could fill? It was crazy. Too little time. I was too young to work at the consulate and it would have been obvious what I was doing. Sweeping churches. Ringing bells? Driving tourist carriages? I had to complete my degree."

"I have your letters," he said. His sadness cut through me.

I watched a goose and seven ducks glide by, their feet churning while their bodies remained calm. I was churning. Anything but calm.

"It may surprise you." I looked at him. "I have your letters, too. I read them from time to time. Thomas caught me once. He made me read them to him."

"Andreas found them while packing for Lucerne."

"One form of transparency, I guess," I said.

Hansi leaned elbows to knees, "He already knew about you. I demanded openness from him. I had to do the same."

"What was he like?"

He turned to look at me. Wistful happiness shone on his face.

"Remarkable. Intelligent. Street smart. He was an attorney. The government recruited him to work on a project in Lucerne. I still have no idea what it was. We both worked long hours. We found time; we made time for each other. He knew I loved you. He also allowed me to have room for you alongside him. He once said he knew you were no threat because you'd never come back, and we didn't know where you were. Maybe he was jealous. That was the only time he said anything like that. He was right, though, about you. He waited for me to accept it, too."

"Did you ever come to the States?"

"You mean to look for you?"

"I mean on vacation."

"Never the west coast."

"He looked for me, didn't he?"

"If he did, he never said."

"But no west coast. Hansi, an intelligent man working for the government? He was a spy, my friend."

Our laughter raced across the lake. People on the other side looked up.

I patted him on the back. "You aren't in Vienna!"

"I didn't notice." He sat back and tousled my hair, something he used to do all the time.

"Anna Marie?" I ask.

"I was there last weekend. I am serious about you coming along. I doubt she'll remember you except from comments Mutti used to make around the holidays. We can get a hotel if you are more comfortable with that."

"Your parents talked about me?"

"There's that arrogance they loved so much. They called you their American son, for fuck's sake! I couldn't get away from you. Andreas bore it like a saint. He was surprised they didn't set you a place at Christmas dinner. They always wanted to know when Thanksgiving was so they could toast you with a Stiegl." He shook his head remembering and in disbelief.

"Did your parents know about me?" He sat back for an answer.

"I mentioned you obliquely when I came out," I replied, "Dad died fifteen years ago. Mom last year."

"Two major deaths in three years. No wonder you're a mess."

I stood to stretch then half knelt on the bench looking down at him.

"I'm not a mess, Hansi. Lost and confused. Hurting. Being in a rough spot isn't the same as existential messiness."

"There's that intelligent approach to emotions I loved so much. Let's get into that again!" He patted my knee.

"Is it time for more food?" I said, twisting back to sitting down.

"By the time we walk back it will be," he smiled. "Greyling, I don't see a mess. I see a struggle. Let me help."

"I'm going back into counselling when I get back," I stretched the truth. I scheduled a meditation retreat on the coast, the part where the Pacific Ocean slams violently into the upthrust of the North American tectonic plate, anticipating that sound and fury would dislodge whatever needed a swift kick for motivation. Salzburg wasn't doing the trick this time around.

"Can we avoid Augies?" I lolled my head to stretch the tightness in my neck, shoulders, and upper back.

"You didn't meet anyone new last night. Maybe start there?"

"Last night?" I looked around the lake. "At the top of the annals of weird."

Hansi said, "I must speak with Rheinhardt about inviting people to someone else's party."

"You didn't invite Gunther?"

"I told you, Sam. Gunther and I have not interacted much for decades. I tolerated the intrusion."

"Does he always have a retinue of young men?"

"Money grubbers. Which way do you want to walk back? Maxglan?"

"Seems he is a testament to the movement of the social classes," I said.

"If you ascribe to American style capitalism."

"Listen to you. Still the rebel fighting for the underdog." I pushed his shoulder. His smile of youth graced his face. "You were always so damn cute when you went political and almighty savior." I grinned and stood.

"Maxglan it is," he said, not responding to my jibe.

Avoiding joggers and dog walkers, we took the long way around the lake. The glorious blue sky contrasted with the green forests and grey granite. Birdsong filled the air unraveling a few of the mysteries of Mozart's inspiration.

"Do you?"

"Do I what?" I responded.

"Fight for the underdog?"

"I'm an attorney. I am not rich. You tell me."

"Poor attorneys can be assholes," he stumbled aside to let a jogger with a dog rustle by. He grabbed my neck to steady himself. I caught him before he fell.

"Steady there, mein Schatz," I said. I blinked astonishment.

He carried on as if he hadn't heard my endearment. "Of course, I cannot judge if you were an asshole attorney. I suspect not."

We walked another three hundred yards in silence.

"You owe me dinner," I said grabbing his shoulders and shaking him.

"How is an American burger chain?"

"Europeans love us and hate us at the same time."

"Sometimes in the same restaurant."

My enjoyment of his laugh and humor bubbled to the surface from a long-ago reservoir. I held him from behind and squeezed.

"American exceptionalism is on the march!" He roared, freed himself, then took off in a semblance of a run toward Schloss Leopoldskron.

I jogged after, catching up when he sat on a bench next to the paved path. As I slowed, I stepped to the side to avoid a fast walker, one of those guys with the swerving hips like the ones who used to close the Olympics as the final event on the last day.

The smell of dog shit filled the air.

"The fragrance of exceptionalism!" He laughed loud enough to startle the ducks, geese, and swans on the lake.

"So funny—" I started to remove my walking shoe.

"Clean it in the lake," he pointed to the edge of water where grass and reeds met.

"Damn dog owners," I muttered.

"You never had a dog?"

"Yes, we had a dog." Exasperation stumbled with me to the lake. "No, I wasn't perfect in cleaning up after him. I know that's where you were going. Rebel rebel." I found a stick and scrubbed shit.

"Tell me about Thomas."

"I did. Over brunch."

"That was the public relations summary."

I shook my head. "The fact that I loved him is all you get." I returned to the path avoiding smears of dog doo but not the odor. "You loving the stench?" I asked.

"It was your twerking ass that mesmerized me."

I turned to start a real twerk in his face and he pushed me away. I recognized the older couple coming our way and pretended to tie my shoe instead.

"Haben noch einen schönen Tag," I said as they passed, unsure if they recognized me or touted me as another rude American. They snorted past, with a glance toward Hansi.

"Let's go." Hansi pushed me as he stood. "You know that couple?"

"The old guy pushed me aside with his walking stick up on Kapuzinerberg the other day."

"He is the retired conductor of the Salzburg Festival Orchestra. She is his lead soprano."

"Helpful knowledge the next time I fend him off."

"They are quite delightful when you take the time."

"Perhaps if he didn't assault people."

"Greyling, you have the time to get to know a few other people."

"I met Rheinhardt. I am on a shouting-booze-orders kind of relationship with a barman. Georg Stohl spies on me at the hotel. Gunther is back in my life. I have you. How many 'people'," I used air quotes as a shield of sarcasm, "does one tourist need?"

"A 'tourist,'" he shot the air quotes back at me, "can relax and hang with some guys. American exceptionalism could be set aside for the duration of your 'visit'."

"You've made your point—again," I stopped while he continued to walk.

I looked up at the back side of Hohensalzburg. The ugly side, in my opinion. The staid and solid side. The side that rebuffed all assaults. The small, modern, metal and glass restaurant protruded over the valley. From this point of view, it was an odd extension. It intruded on history. Today it seemed like a mistake.

I quickened my pace to catch up.

Before I could say anything, he said, "I think I will leave for Vienna."

I stepped in front of him putting my hand up.

"Halt," I said. I took his hand in mine. "I can't do what you want, Hansi. I'm not here to rekindle anything with you or even this city. I can't."

His hand dropped to his side. His head drooped. "I'll say hello to my mother for you. She will be happy to know you returned," he started walking again.

"I thought she was—"

"She's in a home. Anna Marie visits us when she can. She is spry and alert. Anna relieves me from time to time. Mutti asks about you at the holidays. She still toasts you for Thanksgiving, probably as a way to stay in touch with Vatti. She will be happy to know you have returned."

"I know what you are doing, Hansi."

"No, you do not, Sam! But I will tell you here on this path with strangers passing by."

"Please, I—"

"What I am doing is trying to cope. Of all people you should know that three years isn't time enough to grieve. I left Lucerne to return to where my friends are. To help Mutti and be closer to Anna. You may think I have a glorious life here because Salzburg for you is a place of magic. A place of discovery. Coming of age. A place of adventure for a year that may or may not have trapped you in a love affair that won't go away. Sam, magic must die. Adventures must end. Only then can you go home. Magic died when you left. My adventure died when Andreas died. I came home to find myself. Then you appeared. The adrenalin of magic rose up like Charlemagne arising from the Untersberg to save Europe from itself. The magic of hope is what you brought with you. Once again, I learn the hard way that hope is the last great despair and magic ends. Greyling, I live on the edge of despair cleaning shit from my shoes every day. I revisit the places we loved, looking to touch the love I had—you or Andreas, it doesn't matter which because you are both the loves of my life. Coping is what I am doing, mein Schatz."

He looked across the lake towards the Untersberg rising above the valley, late afternoon rays of light forming between its crags. He looked at me. I wilted, as I always had when he did that.

Before I could say anything, he stepped around me and walked toward Leopoldskronstrasse.

"Hansi," I shouted after him.

He raised his arm, wagged an upraised index finger at me, then waived his hand to say goodbye.

"Hansi," I said with less umpf. He looked both ways for traffic then crossed the street disappearing behind the greenery of the grounds of the Schloss.

I weaved my fingers behind my neck and bent down, a sickness forming.

"Haben noch einen schönen Tag," escaped my lips along with the sadness that had overcome me.

I didn't move very far. I asked the maître d' at the Schloss if they served afternoon tea, which I knew they did but my reeling brain couldn't recall or was using a feigned ignorance as a coping strategy.

Sitting on the patio at a table for two, I contemplated the lake, a goose followed by seven ducks, and the shit I needed washed off my shoe when I returned to the hotel. Magic. Adventure. Dying hope. I looked at my phone wondering if my travel agent would pick up on a Sunday that would be 8:00 a.m. her time. I slipped it back into my front pocket, patting it to feel connected to anyone other than Hansi.

Tea and cakes must have tasted of something. My cup and plate were both empty.

It was equidistant to walk through Neutor and the tunnel rather than the way we had come through Nonntal. I wanted to avoid Zecha and the early-to-work Rheinhardt who might see me walking by.

The cool of the tunnel was a relief before emerging into the tourist zone. I took a side few steps into the cemetery at St. Peter's to poke around with the dead, which seemed to be the theme of the afternoon. Cemeteries had a way of stimulating my senses. After thirty minutes I ambled among the remaining tourists in Domplatz and Residenzplatz toward my hotel.

Concierge Georg darted after me, envelope in hand.

"Sunday not your day off, Herr Stohl?" I said with a genuine smile.

"Summer. Too much to do."

"Can't wait for winter, then?"

"It will come soon enough," he said as the lift doors closed on his smile.

I tossed the envelope onto the bed and went to pee. I changed into kinder clothes.

The bounce of the bridge felt familiar. I paused briefly to watch the Salzach's summer flow. As I entered what had become my new bar, the barman lifted my bottle, or maybe a new one I was about to start. I learned his name. Frederic. Fred for his closest customers. Over three fingers of dark magic I got to know another person, who was fond of fucking older tourists, particularly of the American exception. Air quotes wafted through my brain. I did not latch onto them or snigger at their insignificance. Fred might be a good adventure was what lingered through the evening.

Six

Fred lounged on the bed beckoning me back, which I had done twice before this encouragement. I sat in the chair glancing between the brick-built bartender and the staid, solid fortress on top of the hill.

"You said you are from Klangenfurt, nicht wahr?" I said, not bothering to look toward the bed.

"I told you that when you were very drunk, Sam."

"I am a smart drunk, Fred," I replied. "Why Salzburg?"

"Serious after sex, too."

"You could be in Vienna. Or Berlin. Barcelona. Ibiza. Some exotic Greek island."

He motioned to the bed for what would clearly be the last time because he was tiring of the game.

"I'm not good at languages," he said.

He shifted his legs off the bed, stretched the rest of his muscles, and stood, naked to the breeze flowing in from the open windows. He twirled around hard as a ship's mast, and that was just his torso.

"Shower?" he said stretching his luck.

"Done. Waiting for you," I said, looking out the window, noticing for the first time that rooms across the courtyard were being cleaned and prepped for the next bunch of tourists. I felt like I had moved in for the duration.

I walked to the bathroom door and shouted over the water, "Am I taking you to breakfast?" I had to knock on the glass door to get his attention.

"Danke, nein."

I was relieved. He is good in bed. A great barman. Amazing to look at. Not the best company for conversation, although with some work I suspected he had the balls to go far in life. I liked Fred but this fling would be our last. I hoped he wouldn't spit in my single malts.

Herr Stohl picked up on the first ring.

"Is that for two, Herr Greyling," he said after I requested a new breakfast joint.

"Nur eins," I replied with enough pique that I was certain he got my message. No 'bitte' at the end of the sentence to soften the blow.

Fred started to sing in the shower. Something Thomas always did. Tenors both. Similar timbre with a miniscule vibrato at the end of held notes. He was coaxing an aria I recognized from *The Marriage of Figaro*, an exquisite choice for his range. Thomas wasn't as good.

I sat on the bench at the end of the bed. He stepped out still drying off.

"You have a lovely voice," I said.

"More than a good fuck then," he smiled. "I'd suggest spending the day together, but I am taking the train to Munich for a voice lesson. You could come with me if you don't mind hanging out for two hours by yourself."

"Nice thought," I said. "I have plans." I wondered why I kept lying in these situations.

While Fred dressed, I opened the envelope from the night before.

Fuck. Fuck. Fuck.

No phone number to call to decline. Not wanting to call Georg so as not to tip off Fred, I decided to ignore the invitation. I ushered Fred out with a peck on the lips.

A few minutes later when I approached the concierge desk, Fred was there talking with Georg. The specter of small-town gossip reared its ugly head. They both chortled then looked at me. At least it wasn't look at me then laugh, I thought. Small consolation.

Fred excused himself with another peck on my lips. Privacy be damned.

"I am told, Herr Greyling, that a car is to pick you up at noon."

"Right," I replied. "First, call me Sam. Second, would you please politely cancel that car and those arrangements. I would appreciate both."

"I am unable to do either, Herr Greyling." He closed his over-sized appointments calendar with a thud. "I hope you understand."

"No, I don't, Georg. You told me when I arrived that you are here to serve the guest. Call me Greyling, then. Please cancel the afternoon or whatever Gunther has planned for me." I turned and walked out of the hotel.

He ran after me. "Your breakfast reservation, Herr Greyling."

"I'll find a café," I reeled around, yelled in his general direction, and strode toward the river.

In the back reaches of my mind, I feared Gunther would track me down. I needed to nip this in the budding nightmare it could become. Our interactions way back then were fraught and difficult. I couldn't call it friendship by any stretch of the imagination. His propensity for control and conceit were apparent then, even before he had whatever level of wealth or income disparity he tossed around now.

I bounced over the footbridge aiming to saunter through the Mirabell neighborhoods and perhaps avoid the choices either Gunther or Hansi would consider obvious for me to make. I found a small, student-filled Konditerei piping classical music onto the street. I was by decades the oldest person there but not a single head turned or conversation paused for my entry, ordering, or finding a seat. I relaxed with a few minutes of unobtrusive deep breathing. I avoided pulling out the tourist map but did open the Mozarteum listings to see if any daytime concerts might be happening—on a Monday. Doubtful.

The woman in the couple next to me said, "Excuse me, sir, are you American? I am sorry to intrude."

Engage or politely disengage. That was the question flopping in my head.

"It shows?" I smiled. Their laugh told me this was not a new response for them to hear. "Sorry, yes, I am. Visiting old haunts."

"Do you enjoy the Mozarteum?"

"Anyone who doesn't is an idiot," I said, a tad too loud even in a full café.

"There are no concerts today."

"Yeah, Mondays in Europe. Are you students of music? American students?"

"Toby is studying piano and voice. I am studying violin and conducting," said the young woman.

"How exciting!"

They delighted at my enthusiasm. "You should come to our recital tonight. It's our year-end performance so not technically a concert." Toby chimed in. "Lynda is first violin in our ensemble. Leads and plays. I'm on piano tonight."

"Thank you for the offer but I have plans." These lies have got to stop.

"The Saal is quite large for our meager audience. Bring your friends with you," Lynda said. I couldn't tell if she was fighting performance anxiety or disappointment that her base of support was smaller than she had hoped.

Out of politeness I added a date in my phone calendar with time and place. I said I'd try to be there. Is a half lie in fact a full lie? My conundrum of the day.

Toby and Lynda excused themselves.

I nursed my black Americano with two sugars thinking that it isn't that hard to meet new people even at my age. Defying

Hansi's taunt. Except, to classify as friend I'd have to go to the recital and take them out for a drink afterwards and get to know them. I realized I hadn't learned if they were American. They could be Canadian. It didn't matter. I decided I'd show up and hope for a relaxing evening, whatever happens.

The nearby newspaper rack had an international English publication on the top rung, with three German papers stacked beneath, followed by a French rag of some sort. I grabbed the local paper, the Salzburger Nachrichten, and did my best to focus on reading, which was the lesser skill I developed when learning the language. I was great at speaking and conversation. I was okay at writing because: German grammar. Reading was always a struggle for me with eyes darting to the end of sentences to find the verb to try to force sentence structure into an English construct. I persisted through several stories of Austrian politics, southern German social gossip, and Salzburg cultural news.

When I turned to page four, I sat back in my seat. My head tweaked involuntarily to one side. My lower face contorted a frown. The headline read, *"Local man donates generous sum to local charity."*

The photo dominating above the fold was of Hansi smiling over an oversized check with lots of zeroes and a large first number, being handed to two people said to be the CEO and CFO of a major health charity. His smile sucked me into the frame. It was forced, unlike the two other sets of teeth bared with excitement and gratitude. Rather than thinking 'Good on you!', I thought, what are you doing if you aren't happy about it.

My instinct was to call Hansi to let him know I had seen the article. Congratulations were in order. Calling now would be unseemly as he might assume a change of heart based on his donation, which indicated he was modest about his position in life and in Austrian society. Unless I was assuming too much.

That was a possibility, of course, because I have a habit of assumptions when it comes to Hansi. It would seem.

Perhaps I could lie by omission and not mention the article. Tourists don't tend to read local newspapers, especially in native languages. He'd know I might, and that Concierge Georg Stohl might have drawn my attention to the article.

I wanted to invite him to the recital. He was my only option other than going alone. Rheinhardt, I supposed. Then Gunther would know and want to intercede. Going alone or not at all. Two options only.

I abandoned the newspaper and the café to wander up Linzergasse looking in shop windows, raising questions about who buys this expensive stuff, and would I buy it if I cared anymore. There were some beautiful items beckoning the willing through the doors. Shop keepers hustled and bustled to open on time. A few early, elderly shoppers trundled in the direction I was headed. A small couple ahead caught my eye. They also saw me. They stopped discreetly looking at high-end street fashion that only wealthy teens and twenty-somethings would dare to purchase much less wear in public.

I sauntered up to the same window and chuckled.

"Guten morgen," I smiled my reflection at the locally famous musicians, "I can see both of you wearing these items to your next concert."

The old conductor playfully struck my leg with his stick.

"Ouch!" I feigned. "Your multiple beatings remind me of the Krampus I encountered decades ago when I was a student here."

She leaned past her husband, "When you first knew Hans Wortmann, nicht wahr?"

"He told you. How kind of him."

"He told you of us, Herr Greyling," she reprimanded with a wink and grin fit for arts royalty.

"I apologize for my rudeness the other day," I said turning toward them, knowing not to touch shoulders to indicate sympathy.

"No need. You are American, after all." Her laugh was an elegant soprano. His, a sumptuous baritone.

"Austrians must be sick of us," I said.

"Much of Austria appreciates your money. We don't appreciate that insipid film." The three of us roared agreement.

"Are you shopping or merely looking," I said.

"Our daily walk is all," she said.

"I am being rude again. My name is Sam Greyling."

"We know. Hans told us."

I waited for them to introduce themselves. I was not clear on Austrian social constructs. I didn't ask even though my rude American credentials had been affirmed. Perhaps they assumed Hansi had told me. Awkward.

"May I walk with you?"

"No, Herr Greyling. This is our time alone. Together." They looked at each other and nodded. "Would you join us this evening for some music?"

This time I would not be lying. "Thank you. I have an engagement. Perhaps another evening?"

"Hans told us you would say that." She laughed and smiled. "He knows you well, nicht wahr?"

"Quite well, it would seem." I returned the smile but not the laugh. "However, I am committed this evening. May I host you for lunch or dinner later in the week?"

"Aren't you joining Hans in Vienna?"

"You know so much," I said. Brow furrowed in consternation. Head banging in consternation.

"Andreas was our son. Hans is also our son."

There's me told.

"Sorry, I did not know," I offered.

"He said you'd say that, too." She did not smile or laugh.

The old man wrote in a notepad he freed from his trouser pocket. He handed a page to me.

"We no longer stay out late. Perhaps supper at our home on Wednesday?" he said. She squeezed agreement on his arm. They turned and shuffled up the Gasse, the route I would no longer be taking. I watched them peer into windows like school kids searching for sweets. They disappeared around the bend before I turned back toward Altstadt.

Days without plans create their own narratives. The story of this day was turning into a doozy. It wasn't even lunchtime.

Coincidental friendships were popping up all over the place. Before I knew it, I'd feel right at home again. Oh, I saw what Hansi was doing. And Gunther. I wondered if they were in cahoots. I dismissed that as paranoia.

Yet, paranoia intact I didn't want to return to the hotel. Georg and Gunther were in cahoots. I'd have to go back to change for the recital. Recitals in Salzburg require a certain amount of respect. My tourist jeans and shouty t-shirt would not be acceptable even in our modern relaxed world. Passing through the lobby would alert the duo to send a car and to whisk me off to who knows where for what with whom. Avoidance until the last minute was in order.

I slunk through passageways back into St. Peter's cemetery and plopped my tiring butt on a stone-cold bench. I couldn't hide in religious institutions for six hours. I'd be a drunken mess if I stowed away in pubs for the duration. My unplanned narrative turned from a sweet morning of delight to a sour mash of yuck.

"It is forbidden to sit there," said the gardening monk, looking like one of the potbellied dwarves of Mirabell. He tsked his shears my direction then returned to grooming the nearby grave of a long dead Salzburger or besainted confrere.

"I am sorry," I stood to leave. "Father," I said to the hunched man, possibly fifty but who knew when monks were involved.

"Brother," he said as he straightened and twisted his creaks away.

"Father, why do people lie?"

He scratched his head with his shears.

"Sir, for that you must ask a psychiatrist."

"The Church must have something to say."

"I am not the Church and have little to say."

I respected his humility but suspected his own lie. "You are seen as a voice of the Church." I could have gestured to his dirt-stained habit but refrained from subtle mockery.

"Seen but not heard. I have work to complete before Sext. Please excuse me." He knelt back down to pull at weeds and trim lower on the bush he was tending.

At first, I heard 'sex' instead of the liturgical hour of monastic midday prayer. I chuckled and turned away.

I turned back, "Father—Brother. Do you allow guests for prayer and meals?" Great place to hide I was thinking. And how many tourists get to do that.

"The Office is boring unless you know Latin. Our noon meal is weak on protein. There are better options out there." He waved in the direction of the secular world.

"You would not make a very good tourist guide, Brother," I said.

"Thank God for small favors. Now go away."

I went away. Out the gate. Back into the world where sex means sex and Sext is alien.

I started thinking about the goulash I didn't have a few days ago. Good option, and dining in a Hungarian themed restaurant would kill thirty minutes or so. If I could find one without the help of Georg. I skirted my street into the back passages behind the cathedral not going as far as Nonntal. There used to be a great Hungarian joint in this vicinity. I started my search.

Not fifty steps into my journey there it was. Founded 1857. Looking the same as my last visit.

I settled in, ordered the house specialty, ate some bread, and downed the goulash in minutes. All the flavors of a nation came back. I followed it with a wheat bier that complemented it perfectly, the strong flavors of paprika melded with the softness of the gentle brew. I left satisfied but with five hours to hide.

I chanced it for a nap.

I flitted through the lobby when not one employee was on point. Rare but fortunate.

I unplugged the phone. Madness. A security problem. The audacity. I laughed out loud.

Turns out I needed a nap. Fred must have worn me out more than I thought. I awoke at 5:00 p.m. As I sauntered toward the shower, I noticed an envelope on the floor. Cleanliness was first in line. I stepped over it when I walked out the door in a smart suit complemented with bright sneakers. A true street fashionista if ever.

Concierge Stohl entered my field of vision. It was a physics question as to who would reach the door first. He won, blocking my way in a genteel militaristic manner.

"Herr Drecker would like a word, Herr Greyling. He happens to be on the phone at the moment. Would you like to take the call at my desk or on a house phone."

I stepped around him.

"Herr Stohl, Herr Drecker can go fuck himself."

Georg stepped aside in a huff.

I ducked into Zipher again for a quick Semmleknodelsuppe und noch einmal bier. Perfect to be on time for the 7:00 p.m recital near the Mozarteum. I was excited to hear what Toby and Lynda would perform. I might have asked but in my lazy morning mood I failed in that regard.

On my way over the Salzach, I pondered my monkish question about lying. Not the existential version but a specific to me inquiry. I realized the answer was simple and clear. It went back to something Hansi had said a few days before. Fear. Fear of being known, and specifically by someone I might hurt or who could hurt me, i.e., like Thomas. And I suspected like Andreas for Hansi.

It had not dawned on me that by dying, Thomas had hurt me. The truth was that I felt hurt by him for abandoning me. He didn't do the hurting. I hurt myself with a Sam-centered view of the world.

I stopped to watch the river swirl around the bridge pylons. A piece of driftwood stuck in the churn as freezing mountain water rushed past its calm resting place. I wondered how long that log had been stuck there. I watched it for too long, seeing myself as the world rushed by, as opportunity poured through the controlled banks of the fast-moving Salzach. Fear holding me in place.

I also noticed the time and took off in a semblance of a run fearing I was now late for a chance to escape my churn.

Brushing my hair back to create a facsimile of nonchalance, I found a single seat on the end of a row, six rows from the front. Fifty or sixty people filled the available seats, although there was room at the back for more rows. A good turn out for a student recital. I didn't have time to look around. Toby, Lynda, and their fellow musicians entered from the rear of the performance space. A trio of strings flanked by the piano. After the requisite welcome and applause, they sat, adjusted instruments and clothing, and floated into their first-half repertoire—a strenuous Beethoven piano quartet, a softer Mozart piece, and solos by each student.

At intermission, I ran to the toilet for the relief I didn't have time for when I arrived. I was grateful I chose a stall rather than a urinal. His voice carried down the long hallway from the performance room to the toilets. His screeching echoed in the tiled chamber in which I would be trapped until he departed. I decided I'd sneak into the recital much as I did an hour ago, doing everything I could to avoid Gunther seeing me.

The second half was as delightful as the first except that I barely heard a sound because I was obsessing with my escape plan. I wanted to speak to Toby and Lynda, and to meet their friends, to tell them what marvelous performers they were. I wanted a beverage from the bar. I wanted world peace and generational harmony!

"I sensed your presence," Gunther said in his most Vader manner, tortured breathing included, probably from the exertion of blocking my way without me seeing or anticipating.

He draped his arm over my shoulder and neck. His five-inch height disadvantage made it uncomfortable for me. His weight disadvantage was the bigger burden.

He adroitly maneuvered me behind a large plant. Through the foliage I spied Toby and Lynda accepting congratulations and glasses of sparkling wine.

"Can I buy you a cocktail?" I asked.

He placed his hand on the small of my back. I shivered as he turned me away from the celebrations.

"You avoid me, Sam. You make fun of me, Sam. You are impolite, rude, and insensitive to my memories, which have been lovely, if faded and tattered. Your return could be wonderful."

"Gunther. You have a place in my memories."

"You always lie when you are cornered. Always did."

"What do you want?"

"To be acknowledged. Respected. Things I did not enjoy from you in the past."

I removed his hand and stepped to leave.

"Does this have anything to do with Hansi?"

"It is curious that he returns followed by your appearance."

"He's from here, Gunther. He returned two years ago. With Andreas gone it is natural he would come home. Why does this bother you?"

"Like I said, respect, acknowledgement that I exist, being equal."

"I'm told you have a lovely mansion, lots of money coming in, and, as I saw at the party the other evening, a gaggle of pretty boys hanging on for the ride."

"Trifles."

"If you want my sincere company, why didn't you join me for dinner at Weissbach? Or pick up a phone to talk to me. Start with a cocktail in the hotel bar. You have always been a drama queen, Gunnar. You may have noticed I don't appreciate drama in my life. So I avoid, and cover up with a lie or two. I am impressed with your success. Moving up socially in Austria cannot be easy. I wonder though how many of your fellow climbers respect you, acknowledge you, or enjoy your company. If you are offended by my little lies, they must thoroughly disgust you with their insincerities."

"Navigating social graces is like breathing. Unlike for you and Hans. For instance, one would never arrive late for a recital then slink into a side chair. One plans an entrance then follows the plan. That is what got me to where I am. Knowing the rules and following them."

I waved across his shoulder at no one because most everyone had left the room.

"Gunther, darling," I gestured toward his face but didn't stroke his cheek, "one doesn't plan friendships. One celebrates them, engages, opens to whatever comes, and enjoys the ride. Unlike you and your gaggle of gays, friendships aren't controlled. That's why Hansi and I dance to the music at hand." I pulled away. "I would like to greet the musicians. Please excuse me."

He fastened his hand to my elbow and pinched.

"I have waited for you to return to Salzburg. I sacrificed my life for you."

"You built a fiefdom while you waited. I doubt you thought of me until Hansi returned home."

"My kingdom can be yours. I will share it with you. Everything, except one or two of my boys."

I unhinged his hand pushing him aside.

"Leave me alone, Gunther. I didn't return for you."

The heat from his stare bore into my back. Toby was returning to tidy the performance space. I spun him round and said, "Introduce me to your friends."

"You know Herr Drecker?"

"Yes, I do." An unknown punctation mark attempted to end that inquiry.

"He sponsors Mozarteum students. He's important to us." Toby persisted.

"I knew him years ago. That is all."

His arm shot out across my chest stopping forward movement.

"Sam? Oh my god. You are Sam Greyling!"

A definite twist to the inquiry. We approached Lynda and the other string players.

"Your performance was exquisite, you guys," I enthused in hopes of diverting Toby's trajectory.

"This is the Sam we told you about. He's Drecker's muse! This is *that* Sam Greyling."

"Wait. What? Muse?"

Lynda hugged me, "You are all he talks about when he inspires us to discover what is hidden in the music."

"Wait. What?"

"If we'd known we would have invited you to the stage."

What the fuck—. Can it get any weirder? I squelched that thought to stanch any potential of the universe playing tricks. "Yeah. No. That would never happen." Not bothering with further introductions, I thanked them for the evening, extended my apologies, and scampered through the thinning crowd. I glanced back to see them nattering in my direction with Gunther standing square in the middle of the doorway to the performance space. His sardonic frown pushed me faster onto the street.

Monday night after a recital that turned a tad macabre, if macabre could be so twisted. A Krampus of bizarre was beating my brain. Sticks and stones break things. Being someone's secret pocket muse and thus worshipped by said someone's cult was stressing me out.

If I went back to the hotel, I'd have to deal with one of the cult leaders. Georg Stohl was too enthused with getting me together with Gunther. I needed to avoid that scene, especially tonight.

The top of Getreidegasse gave me some comfort. At this hour and this day of the week most of my go-to drinking establishments would be closed, closing, or shouting the German equivalent of last call.

I rang the buzzer for Hansi's apartment. Escaping the Gunther cult for my own muse didn't strike me as twisted in the slightest. I looked up and down the street. A few tourists stumbled toward their hotels. A cleaning crew was slowly making its way this direction. Haydn wafted out a distant window to soften the warm evening.

I rang the buzzer a second time. The door opened mechanically. I rushed into the hallway and looked up. Jogging trousers and slippers greeted me.

"It is rude of me at this hour. Can we talk?"

"You might have assumed I am fucking someone."

"You'd have been right to not open the door, then."

"Clever. How many fingers of scotch is this talk?" His lightness and ease comforted me. By the time I reached the upper landing a glass of dark and luscious greeted me in all its neatness. I took a healthy swig.

In the living room, he bookmarked the tome he had been reading. He brought his own glass of scotch to the sofa.

"Sit," he invited. "Unexpected. Welcome. What are we to discuss?"

I sipped the second finger.

"What are you reading?" I ran a peek over the bit of his library visible in his reading light.

"Are we starting a book club?" He rested his arm on the back of the sofa, drink in that hand. It reminded me of a painting I had seen in some museum somewhere.

"I recall you loved Twain and Steinbeck."

"Devoured them," he smiled his memory.

"Now?"

"Irish. Joyce. Heaney. Doyle. A few others." He sipped his drink. "You didn't buzz my door to talk literature, Greyling. What happened?"

The pillow I stuck behind my aging back didn't support what needed supporting. I moved it out of the way. I leaned against the sofa arm and stretched.

Hansi started laughing.

"What?" I asked.

He shook his head in amusement. "You are so predictable," he smiled.

"Stretching is all," I said settling down.

"Start talking, I go to bed soon."

My head hair felt tired as I ran my fingers through it multiple times. "Gunther thinks I am his muse," I said turning to face him.

"Why is this news?" Hansi set his drink on the table. "He was obsessed with you in our youth. Every time I saw him when I came home, he would talk about it. It was sad and I told him every time."

"I have never been a muse before," I said.

"Do you think being Gunther's muse is something special? Do you think you are special? If I had a euro for every one of his muses."

"That's harsh, Hansi." I picked up an Italian magazine, considered it, and tossed it back on the table. "I think I'm in shock. I rarely thought about *him*. Having him come on so intensely is unexpected. Weird. Unsettling."

"Unwanted?" He nailed it.

"Oddly, I'm a little flattered—,"

He reached out and grabbed my arm before his first guffaw entered my ear.

"Don't mock," I chortled back. "It's nice to know someone thought about me for decades, when I couldn't give a shit." The loudness of my laugh folded into his.

After we calmed down, he said, "His obsession is not your responsibility." He took my drink to refill it. "Four? Three? Two? It's getting late."

"Surprise me. Do you read all this stuff in their languages?"

"Only four languages. Andreas had seven he spoke fluently, and four or five others he taught himself when we went on vacation. I'm a lightweight."

My drink had an ice cube floating unwelcome in it.

"Slows your encroaching drunkenness," he said as he sat back down adjusting his shirt.

I slurped the cube of cold into my mouth and sucked it until I could chew it. Single malt is best at room temperature. The illuminati know this.

"I saw a photo of you."

He sipped his refreshed drink. He did not reply.

"I was surprised, is all. Not to be crass but that's a lot of money."

He laughed, "And you want to know how I came by it."

"It's none of my business."

"That is correct. But the article spelled it out. You fixated on the check, right?"

"It is a large number—"

"To some."

"Now you are being arrogant and circumspect."

"It took this long to sort out Andreas' estate. It was his wish."

I offered an Italianate gesture of 'and', more than hinting I'd like more information.

"Greyling, we both worked very hard. We invested wisely. I inherited from my parents. It all adds up to a comfortable life."

My curiosity stuck to my face.

"We never lived ostentatiously. We saved. It worked out."

"Your comments about Gunther and this place?"

"It is not a competition, mein Schatz. I can call you that now, can I not? At least I know you didn't return for my money."

"Joyce isn't as hard to read as they say," I changed the subject to try to find the right words in this awkward situation. "Except *Finnegan's Wake*, which frustrated and beguiled me."

"We have that in common as well," he smiled.

I slouched against the back of the sofa. Our glasses clinked as I stretched my arm.

"It might be a competition for Gunther," I said.

"He has much more than me," Hansi's index finger stroked my glass. I watched him do it.

"He spends it at a faster clip," I observed.

"It doesn't seem to stop his money grubbing," a tone of contempt nudged in.

"I don't think he's changed all that much. Still needy. Still fearful. Still alone." I touched his finger.

"He has never taken the opportunities sitting squarely in front of him." He sat up, elbows on knees. He tweaked his face in my direction. "You don't need to save him, Greyling. You like saving puppies. He is what he is."

"The thought never occurred to me." I chugged my scotch and fingered my mouth to catch a final taste.

"Do you think you have changed?" He turned toward me.

"I have my idiosyncrasies. One doesn't lose loves and friends and not be affected by the grief of that. One doesn't build a life then have it snatched away and not be changed. My values are deeper and more thoughtful because of it. You may not believe it because of how I have acted these few days, but I have grown up. I have faults, too, ones Thomas coaxed me away from, but he didn't succeed. That makes me sad because I can be a better person. He didn't get to see that happen."

"You aren't predictable, then? Your return hasn't brought the worst out?"

I scootched to his end of the sofa and wrapped my arm around his neck. My scotch splashed a little on his face. I licked it off. He dropped his neck away and into his shoulders.

"Ick. That's disgusting." He sniggered.

"I said your name once during sex," I sniggered back.

"Once? Andreas asked me if I wanted him to change his name!"

"That's sad."

"But sweet that he'd ask, right?"

"No!" I sat back against the sofa. "He must have been a wonderful man."

"Maudlin is a new thing for you, Greyling. Get a grip, mein Schatz."

He moved to his reading chair. My arms rested on the sofa in the warm spot he left behind.

"Your in-laws invited me to supper."

"I know."

"Will you be there?"

"Vienna calling."

"I leave next week," I reminded him.

"Extend your stay. Move in here."

I bolted upright. "What? We aren't exactly hitting it off in case you haven't noticed."

"Nervousness, Sam. Mutually tentative exhaustion. Fear—in case you haven't noticed."

"What do you have to be afraid of, Hansi? Comfort. Money, as I learned today for the first time. Family. Salzburg. I doubt you are afraid."

"Of getting it right. I am, Greyling. The ease of what we had and might again. That is daunting."

"Whoa. Wait. What. Don't get ahead of whatever this is."

"If you walk away this time, we will never see each other again. Surely you know that."

"I can visit. You can come to the States. There's more to do there than here."

"You leave next week. I'll extend my visit to Anna Marie. Accept it, mein Schatz."

"I don't recall you being this manipulative, Hansi. Andreas—"

"Andreas has nothing to do with it, Sam. This is about you and me. I want you to stay. You want to leave. It's that simple."

"What about all those years in between?"

"They don't matter."

"What about how I left you?"

"Are you listening? It doesn't matter?"

I slapped both sides of my face. I ran all my fingers through my hair. I dragged my hands down my face.

Did it matter? Of course, it mattered. I had friends back home. I had a home back home. There were visas for that. There would be stuff to figure out. There'd be stuff to get rid of. There was Thomas to let go of. Of course, it mattered. Head reeling and heart roiling were two of many things happening and mattering.

I looked at him watching me from the scant light of his library lamp. The bemused upturn of his lips beguiled like the stream of consciousness of Irish writers of yore. Intrigue. Challenge. Patient. Humor. Hot.

"We don't know each other," another tactic spewed out of me.

"Yes, we do."

"You may think you do. I don't know you. You're a mystery."

"My life was plastered all over the newspaper this morning. My in-laws invited you to supper. What are you afraid of, Greyling?"

"Failing. Rejection. Being marooned in Austria. Discovering the truth."

"You can always go back to America. Tourist visas last for ninety days. We're picking up where we left off years ago. We have other memories, too. Those aren't going anywhere. We are making new ones. It's that simple, Sam."

"I knew you were doing this. I told you I knew what you were doing."

"You buzzed my door tonight. You—."

"Because of Gunther."

"You could have gone to Augies and got drunk. You could have gone to dinner at Zecha. You could have had room service in the hotel. You came here. Don't create excuses where there are none. Greyling, I know you. This is why you came back."

"The truth? I came here to escape Thomas."

He sat forward, shifting the light that now illuminated him from behind like a guru. I cringed at what I'd said and what I suspected was coming. I downed two fingers of dark malted rye.

He said, "You came here to embrace love, Sam. You are so lucky. We are so lucky. Two deep loves in our lives. Embrace Thomas. You can't escape him anyway. He's a part of you, like Andreas is a part of me. That is good, and right, and wonderful. Since you ask so many questions of me, let me tell you that I struggle with embracing Andreas loosely so I can live my life without the crushing grief. I can hold him and waltz with him. And I can let him stay here in a place of memories while I got out to meet other people. That party was the first time I've had anyone into my home since he died. It was brutal for me, and not because Rheinhardt overstepped by inviting Gunther."

"And me," I chimed in.

"Yes, and all of Gunther's boy toys. I hid in the bedroom until I heard your voice. You brought me out of avoiding what I had done." He sat back into his chair and the more flattering light. "I don't know what I would have done that night if you hadn't come." He covered his mouth to hide the tremor of his chin and lips.

"How many fingers you want? Three. Two. What will help," I said gathering our glasses. "No ice, though."

He chuckled and wiped his eyes.

I dangled his two fingers of liquor in front of him. "What would you have done if I hadn't returned to Salzburg? That was the greater possibility." I sat on the floor leaning against his chair, one arm encircling his leg. In sipping my drink, I remembered that we used to sit like this when contemplating our future options. One of us at the foot of the other. "You introduced me to single malts. Do you remember?"

"You didn't resist, if you recall."

"Such a grown-up drink. Were we grown up back then? Pretending maybe? Trying it on for size, I suppose."

He pushed his leg against me. "Are you saying our love was juvenile?" He touched my hair.

"You were my first. First love; first tormented loss. I have learned that love doesn't mirror one's physical maturing or dying. I think life is about learning to meld love with life."

"And vice versa?" He nailed my dilemma.

My fingers running around the edge of the glass squeaked. The dried malt tasted sweet in my mouth. He tugged at my scalp slowly twisting my hair. I lolled my head back. A relaxing moan escaped into the room. I turned to lean on his knee, looking up at him looking down at me. "What would you be doing if I weren't here. In Salzburg, I mean?"

"I know what you are doing, mein Schatz," he rested his index finger gently between his closed lips, like he did when he pondered his deepest thoughts.

"Tell me," I said.

"Creating an excuse for not being here after next week. Building a castle to defend myself when you leave." His finger bounced with his thoughts.

I pushed my chin into his leg above the knee.

"Ow!" He pushed me away. "Why do you do such things?"

I rested back on his leg.

He leaned his head back on the chair. His upturned face looked like a Toulouse-Lautrec post-impressionist painting with grotesque shapes and fauvist colors redefining beauty, and probably longing. I sat up to change my perspective.

"I would be in hiding," he said, looking back down at me. "Like you, but in my own home. Hiding from Andreas and life, I suppose."

"You are so confident at times," I ran my hand up the outside of his leg. He pulled away. I walked my fingers back to his knee and massaged the spot I had hurt.

"That is how I avoid things, Sam. I am confident. I am the strong one. I hold it all together. My in-laws need me to do that, you see. Anna Marie and Mom need me to do that. I avoid telling them all to fuck off. To leave me alone. To let me grieve." He took a deep breath. "I think I haven't properly grieved."

"My being here is not helping." I moved to stand.

His hand on my face warmed my cheek. The strokes of his fingers, rough and soft at the same time, traced the tears falling inside of me.

"You are, Greyling. My darling, Greyling." He set his drink down. The slight chill of that hand touching me made me shiver. Or was it because he was touching me as he had done the night before I left, before we made love the last time.

His silken lips traced my mouth. Damp scotch. The pressure of his tongue opened my lips to accept his tenderness. I ran my hand up the inside of his leg and back to his knee. The familiarity was intense and satisfying.

He sat back. I rested on his leg. A tableau of sublimity.

"I should go," I said, barely audible to myself.

"The air would do you good," he said.

I sat up in a huff. "That was a suggestion that you invite me to stay the night."

"I'm not stupid, Samuel Scott Greyling." He pushed me aside, sat forward in his chair, and stood over me, the humbled Cleopatra with Marc Antony lording over me.

"You're throwing me out?"

"I'm delaying the inevitable, mein Schatz." He leaned down and tousled my hair again. I pushed his hand away. He stepped aside so I could stand. He removed the glass from my hand before I could down the last half-finger of dark gold.

"If it's inevitable, why wait?"

"We are not in our right minds," he said in his confident tone, the bass tone of Roman dictator authority. His self-proclaimed voice of avoidance.

"You might not be," I said, trying to eke out some level of indignation.

"It takes two to tango, Greyling. You are too drunk to dance."

He ushered me to the top of the stairs and pulled the lever to open the street level door.

"Maybe it isn't inevitable." I lifted my eyebrows in the indignation I finally located.

"Good night, Sam," he kissed me on the forehead, his lips leaving heat that hurt my heart. "Be careful walking home. There are bartenders skulking about at this hour."

I glanced up to see his legs turning away as the door closed behind me.

Without the tourists and traffic, the city slipped into the quiet of my memories.

Seven

When I was first introduced to Hansi, it had been a stressful week of tests and presentations in philosophy, German, and art. I was nursing a bier in my pub. I wasn't sure I'd done justice to my knowledge of and excitement for each subject, which were my reasons for studying in Europe.

Perhaps I mumbled something vile. Perhaps I slammed my stein too hard on the table.

Either way, my usual political sparring partner, no bier in hand, said, "This should be an interesting discussion."

I snorted something in my half-German, half-English confrontational drinking tone.

He patted my shoulder while his mule arrived carrying four steins. Nearly dropping them, he set them on the table and returned to the bar to get large pretzels, which were a part of our Friday night confabs.

When he returned, Leon poked my side.

"This is Hansi," Leon said.

I looked up but not at him.

"Hello, Hansi," I stuck my hand out. He held it a second or two too long. I pulled away.

"You do not recognize me," he said.

"Should I?"

"It would be a pleasure if you would." He gulped some bier then tore off a piece of pretzel. He did something I had not seen anyone else in any German or Anglo-Saxon country do. He dunked the bite of pretzel in the bier and scarfed it down.

"Should I be disgusted by that?" I asked, looking at him for the first time. "It's you," I blurted.

He poked Leon. "He's as quick-witted as you said."

"You Austrians all look alike." I wished I hadn't attempted humor but there it was, ripe for ridicule, and rightly so.

We each sucked on our steins for a second or two.

"I haven't seen you on Neutorstrasse this week," Hansi said.

"Intense study week," I replied.

Leon said, "I think every university in the world has tests the same week of every year."

"My practicum was last week so I am off for two weeks." Hansi glanced in my direction.

"What are you studying," I asked.

"Medicine. Innsbruck."

"Why aren't you skiing or snow-shoeing. I thought Austrians flocked to the outdoors whenever they could." One month into my study year and I am insulting the locals.

Hansi squared his shoulders toward me, "You may have noticed—" He turned to Leon, "What is his name? He didn't introduce himself."

"Sam Greyling," laughed Leon.

Hansi continued, "You may have noticed merely by looking at Untersberg that there is no snow, Herr Greyling."

"There are still mountains," I stared back at him.

"There are also museums and concerts and trains to Vienna and food to eat and bier to drink." He lifted his stein in toast then defiantly dunked his whole pretzel. It fell apart in his bier. He and Leon roared their surprise and pleasure.

I sulked.

"In fact, Herr Greyling—"

"Call me Sam, bitte." I smiled my biting retort.

"In fact, Greyling, I am going to a performance of Beethoven's Ninth Symphony tomorrow evening at the Festspielhaus. Leon was going to go with me; he can't now." He looked at Leon who choked on his sip of bier.

"No, I can't go now," Leon reinforced.

"We can have Bratwurst and Kraut before the doors open because that is a very Austrian thing to do. You can then walk me home, unless Leon will be out for the evening then we could go to his place in Neutor."

"Yes, go to my place in Neutor. I am not doing anything now so I will go mountain climbing in the dark."

"A very Austrian thing to do," they said at the same time.

I got up to get more bier for myself. They already had their second stein to hand.

When I returned, with my own pretzel, I said, "OK. I'll go. Why not. I'm not going mountain climbing in the dark so what the fuck."

I tore a piece of pretzel, dunked it, and ate it like a local.

"That's actually very good," I smiled. "Salt and hops. Nice combination."

Hansi scooted out of the bench so Leon could go pee, then moved back closer to me so Leon would sit on the end.

"It will be a good performance even though the Philharmonic in Vienna would be better."

"Tell me about Vienna." I leaned toward him wanting to hear his travelogue. His leg stroked mine under the table. "That's subtle," I said, with a chortle for emphasis.

"Greyling, I have not been subtle with you for one minute. Are all Americans so obtuse?"

"That's a large English word," I said, sitting back up.

"That one word is what caught your attention?" he sat up too, because Leon returned.

"Maybe I am. Obtuse. It's unexpected I guess," I said.

Hansi put his hand on my leg nearer my crotch than I was comfortable with. I couldn't pull away. I didn't push him away.

"Expect it then," Hansi said. Turning back toward Leon, he said, "What do you think of that Nixon fella bombing Cambodia like that?"

Off we went into the technicalities of geopolitics and American aggression toward the rest of the planet. They knew more than I did, which set me back further than I was in the weeks leading up to this moment. I had trouble keeping up even though my Germlish was improving by the gulp. If I was going to keep coming here, I'd have to hone my political science and history, two more courses of study that brought me to Salzburg.

My resolve grew as we corrected history, ridiculed Genghis Khan, Ceaușescu, Tito, and every dictator ass known to history, and tore into modern political systems. It was fast and furious and funny and exhilarating and a very good time.

"I gotta go," said Hansi, pushing Leon out of our cubbyhole. "Mutti und Vatti rules tonight."

"I'll walk you home," I said, pushing out my side of the table and swigging the last quarter liter of my fourth stein. I tottered but held my own.

"I'm going mountain-climbing," said Leon in a sardonic tone.

"It's something Austrians do," we all chimed in.

Leon took off over the foot bridge. Hansi and I meandered north on Steingasse.

"Dammit," I said, "I shoulda peed."

"Come on, American, I know a place."

He pushed me into a short, unlighted alley and dragged me far enough back that no one would see us.

"Not here," I protested. "You go ahead. I'll go back."

Hansi whipped out his dick and let loose.

"Oh, what the fuck," I said doing the same.

After cinching back up, Hansi grabbed my shoulders and spun me around. He kissed me hard and deep. My instinct kicked in. I pulled back. His arms around me didn't let me get far away. He persisted but with less force. As I relaxed, we relaxed into pre-cum inducing snogging and enough groping that it was going to be more than pre-cum if we kept going.

He pulled away.

"You're stopping?" I said, still holding his crotch.

"Delaying the inevitable," he said, touching my face and stepping back.

The acrid stench of urine filled my nostrils.

"You come here often," I said, straightening my dishevel.

"When I can't hold back." He cuffed my chin.

We navigated Altstadt and whispered our way up the tunnel until we stood outside his family home. I had a few more blocks to go before our student lodging.

"Are you serious about tomorrow night?" I asked. Now me, the horny one, sticking my hands in my pockets to avoid touching him, and rocking back and forth so his mouth was a moving target that I wouldn't dare attack even in the darkness of Neutor.

"Let's meet at the horse fountain just inside Altstadt," he said. "We can drop into Zipfer for a brat or two."

"What do I wear?" I turned sheepish tourist.

"You OK with coat and tie? Don't bring the cowboy hat and boots. Too obvious. Not sure Beethoven would approve either."

"This is all new to me," I said.

"I figured that out when you insulted Austrians earlier."

A light flipped on in the vestibule of his house.

"You will meet my family one day soon," he said as he touched my shoulder then turned away.

"I will?" My flummoxed voice shattered the quiet.

"You will." He disappeared up the steps and into the house. He paused in the light that backlit him in his Austrian handsomeness.

The next day one of the women of my student group went with me to spend two months of my allowance on a new suit and two ties. I decided my scuffed black wingtips would have to do until my roommate found some shoe polish to brighten them up. I knew nothing about Beethoven's Ninth Symphony and had no way to hone up without scurrying to the Center library. I decided to let it be an adventure. That helped me relax.

I arrived at the fountain at 5:15, a quarter hour early.

Hansi was propped against the far wall watching carriages full of tourists ride through town. He spotted me and walked to the corner of the fountain to greet me with two cheek kisses.

"You have dressed in an Austrian manner," he said, looking me up and down, "Except for those horse hooves you are wearing on your feet. What are those things?" He pulled my trouser legs up to fully enjoy his humor. "I expected an American cut. This is European class, mein Schatz."

"Please don't call me that," I shied. "This is too new."

He slipped his arm into mine.

"It's OK, Greyling." He gripped me tighter.

"Not if my university finds out," I said pulling away. "They'll send me home."

"Do you want to go home?"

"Hard to evaluate after four weeks," I said.

"You've thought about staying already?"

He pushed me aside as we averted running into a dirndled tourist carrying a collectable stein the size of a bus.

"Do you like Zipfer bier?" he asked.

"Haven't had it," I said.

"You've had more than enough time to test all of the local brews. Come on. Let's get you drunk."

"The concert?"

"The best way to listen to this orchestra. I'll take you to Vienna. Friends can get us tickets for the Philharmonic. *That* is classical music."

"What is this?"

"It's still the summer tourist leftovers here, I am afraid. The musicians are tired at this point. The conductor wants the season over. He's being replaced next season. You'll see the difference when we get to Vienna."

He seemed certain of that, and most everything else about us. No red flags flying so far. I must be OK with it all.

"I don't have a school break until Thanksgiving," I said.

"What is that?" His brow crinkled.

We sat at the table nearest the windows and the door. Never my favorite spot. I preferred cubbyholes in dark places.

"When we give thanks for our European ancestors surviving their first harvest in the new world." That would have to do for a history lesson on an ill-fated pilgrim adventure that has been spun into propaganda for nearly four centuries. "It is always a four-day holiday, even for us students abroad."

"Tell me the dates and I'll skip school those days. With trains both ways, four days will not be enough but it's a start. You'll love Vienna."

"I love Salzburg."

He stood to retrieve our biers and Bratwursts mit Senf and Kraut.

"We'll have time for Strudel after the concert," he said with a wink. "If you want."

He asked me about my family, and wanted names, dates and places as far back as I could remember. I wasn't used to someone taking so much interest in me. It was always about school, class content, future plans, where I want to be in five years, ten years, when I retire. It was refreshing to talk about anything but that.

We walked out of the tunnel into Neutor, a new-to-me symphony wafting through my head. We didn't bother with Strudel.

"I hope Leon remembers he is climbing mountains," Hansi said.

"Are you sure about this," I said, knowing I wasn't.

We stopped in the small park just outside the tunnel and he sat me down on the only bench in the park. There was a soldier sculpture pointing to the sky; he looked young and pure and hopeful.

"Greyling, are you a virgin?"

A night owl hooted. A squirrel running on its nighttime clock scampered under the bench to hide.

"Well, no." I lied.

"Don't lie if you are."

"Well, yes. Yes, I am."

"Neither woman nor man?"

"Only myself." I wanted to hide under the bench.

"Lying would make it worse," he said. He crossed his legs. His foot rubbed my shin.

"Maybe Leon doesn't need to climb a mountain now?" I asked, not sure what I wanted.

He sat back, uncrossed his legs, and put his arms on the back of the bench—close enough to touch my shoulder. Although he didn't.

He waited.

"I'm sorry," I said. "I should go."

"Where, Greyling? Where would you go?"

"To my room."

"Alone."

"My roommate might be there."

He knocked the back of my head.

"Ow. Don't do that." I wanted to be upset but only because I was nervous.

"What do you want?"

"I'm sorry, Hansi, I—"

"Don't say that Sam. Don't be sorry for what you think or do. Do what you want when you want it."

"I'm sorry. I'm not sure. What I want."

"I am sure, Greyling."

"One-night stands aren't what I want."

"They aren't for me either. You silly American. In the last twenty-four hours have you not noticed that I want to be with you? Did you not see it a few weeks ago on Neutor? You are too smart to be so dense, Sam."

That's me told.

He rubbed my back and shoulder.

I wondered why I had lied. Twice.

"Hansi," I ventured. "I've had sex. It wasn't very satisfying. I guess you could say I am a virgin to intimacy. I've sucked dick."

He turned toward me.

"What do you want tonight? Leon is mountain climbing. I'd like to have to wash his bedding."

The owl flew off as I laughed. The squirrel darted away.

"Let's do it," I stood, offering my hand to him.

"No regrets no matter what," he said.

"Not yet," I smiled in the dark.

Leon's love nest—a moniker that stuck and for which we paid with many meals and liters of bier—was sparse, as one might expect for a student living alone. It was an oversized studio tacked on the side of a two-story stucco home with its own entrance. Hansi knew where the key was, indicating to my naïve self that he'd done this before. A small red flag appeared at the bottom of a very short flagpole. We'd have to be very discreet given how quietly we scrunched on the gravel driveway. I doubted the owners were fooled.

Windows pointed to the side of Monchsberg. No houses or roads or walking paths. Light from a too-bright yard lamp cast static shadows that didn't help me avoid the furniture that bruised my shins and toes. We kept the lights off.

It was warm enough to throw the duvet on the floor. My head landed on the pillow a mere second before Hansi jumped my bones, albeit gently.

"I won't hurt you," he whispered in a voice I hadn't heard before.

"Good," I said. "Wouldn't want to have to hurt you back."

"Silly American," he said leaning down to nudge my neck on one side and filter my hair through his hand on the other side. I pulled his head back by grabbing his hair.

"Too much," he moaned.

"Sorry," I replied.

"Stop saying that," he poked my side and tickled me up and down my torso, kissing my neck and shoulder.

My nerve endings tingled. My whole body was near to spasm. No longer a virgin to lovemaking, I welcomed Hansi's hands and mouth on my body. I welcomed the probing and shifting that I knew was leading to ecstasy. I let go of thoughts. I embraced fear. I engorged the happiness that was streaming through me.

Between full-on sex, I enjoyed exploring his body even though I could barely see him in the shadows. His body hair slipped across my fingers like delicate cotton threads. His muscles rippled when he moved, like waves of steaming water. His breath was slightly sour from our earlier dinner. The sound of his breathing rasped in my ear. I rattled my hand over his abs and went down on him again. He writhed off the bed. His back arched. He widened his legs. The taste of him lingered in my mouth.

I lay back. He lounged his arm across my gut. We lay this way falling and climbing in and out of sleep. Spent for the moment. Recharging.

"Where does Leon actually go?" I broke the silence.

"Not to worry," Hansi whispered into my chest.

"When does he come back?"

"When he knows we're gone."

"Aren't you on Mutti and Vatti rules?"

"Why the questions, Greyling?"

"Trying to figure it out," I said with no irony.

"Do you need to be somewhere?" He leaned his head onto his crooked hand.

"Roomie will wonder where I am."

"Is he your Vatti?"

"That's not the point, Hansi."

"Leon stays with friends. He's fine with this. Mom and Dad know what I am doing. They know everything. I'm gonna bet your roommate has figured it out, too. Stop worrying."

"Sorry."

"Jesus Christ, Sam." He sat up and leaned against the headboard. "Do you want to be doing this or don't you?"

"Yes," I said. I rolled against him laying my head in his lap. His dick bounced against the weight.

"If you don't want to, let me know now because I am not going to invest in a dead end. Sit up and look at me." His instruction was dictatorial.

"OK, Genghis," I snarked.

"Don't," he said.

"Sorry."

He threw his hands up. "What will it take for you to stop that?"

"Stop what?"

"Apologizing. Not being honest. Hiding in your fear."

"I don't understand why you care so much, Hansi. I'm a foreign student who will leave in a few months. OK, let's have some fun. Don't care so much. It freaks me out."

"I'm scared, too. We won't see each other much. Innsbruck. My family. Your group stuff. We gotta make the most of it."

"You want to plan this thing we're maybe doing?"

"No. I want to acknowledge that it's all possible. That we give each other everything, nothing held back."

"You got into this pretty fast, Hansi. Don't decide by yourself what you want and force me into it. If you think I'm scared now, wait till you keep doing this."

I rolled off the bed to stand at the window, the light flooding my body. He would see a silhouette of my youth. I listened for him to follow.

I stood alone.

When I turned back, he was in the same position with a little more of a lounge against the pillows. The lamplight reached his mid torso with side glow clipping his jaw. His patience stood in contrast to my pushing for an answer.

"If I say no to this, what happens?"

He folded my pillow and crushed it against his furry pecs. I wondered what his family ancestry was. Fair haired. Hairy in the best places. Eyes a shade of blue that matched the color of lakes in the region, not green, not blue, not aquamarine. Dark enough for mystery. Light enough to drown in.

"I go back to Innsbruck and ignore you when I come home. This is my country. I will find someone eventually."

"What do you predict happens to me?"

"You live with regret. Wondering what you missed. Angry that you didn't try. Saddened by your choices."

"You seem so sure," I said, sitting on the foot of the bed.

"After one day I see you are predictable, Greyling."

I moved to the top of the bed grabbing my pillow from him.

"Is certainty the same as being predictable?"

"Mein Schatz, you are anything but certain. You rely on predictability."

"Then why do you care?"

"I saw you with your friends the first day you all arrived on Neutorstrasse. You have some good-looking men in your group. You stood out. To me. My family commented that this year was a crop of American talent. It was my sister who pointed you out. She said, 'the tall skinny one looks interesting. Perhaps he is smart, the way you like smart, Hansi.' We toasted you. I doubt you noticed us. Your eyes were wider than the moon. Your smile and laugh were tentative. I walked to the fence to get a better glimpse of you as you went into your Center through the back door. You looked back at me but not at *me*. Perhaps at your new life. I took a train to Innsbruck the next day to start my medical training. I thought of you every day, curious if she was right about you being smart in the way I like. That is why I care," he said lolling his head on my shoulder.

I looked into the light, ignoring the shadows. "When I saw you in the shop, I remembered you at the fence. You stared at me. I was shocked when Leon introduced us. I am sorry I am so awkward."

He sunk down along my side licking me all the way to my hip. My dick responded.

"You aren't awkward in bed," he laughed, "For a virgin."

He crawled between my legs. He took me in his mouth working his tongue around the head then his silkiness stroked the length of me. Pleasure crept through me at the speed he worked me. When it reached my brain, I exploded into him. He gagged on the amount of cum I released. He sucked me until I was dry and too sensitive to take any more. He rolled onto his side fingering my balls and softening erection.

After recovering my breath, I said, "I hope that is the smart you like because if nothing else I want to explore your brain."

"The romance of Salieri," he laughed.

"Sorry," I said.

"Instead of 'sorry' every time you don't know something try something else, like, oh, I don't know, 'tell me more' or 'I don't know that reference' or 'what the fuck is that.'"

"Is Salieri a person?"

"There you go. Yes, Italian composer at court in Vienna competing with Mozart. Guess who won."

"I don't know."

"Exactly. You don't know because you've never heard of Salieri but you have heard of Mozart."

"I get it. You were being sarcastic and ironic at the same time. You are so funny, Hansi."

"And that, mein Schatz, is the smart of you that I like."

He kissed my dick then pulled himself next to me.

"It won't be just about sex," I said sheepishly.

"I hope not," he said. "Don't get me wrong, you are hot and sexy and appealing and handsome and good at it, now that you have been introduced to it by the best in Austria, but sex is a piece of you. I already know I want all of you."

"I think I should go," I said slipping my feet off the bed to the hardwood floor.

He pulled me back and placed my head in his lap.

"Leon will require payment for a full night, and I have to wash the bedding whether you stay or go," he said.

"He runs a flop house for indigent gay men of Salzburg?"

"No, only me. He already told me he wants a goulash lunch before I leave for Innsbruck."

"I'm a lowly student, Hansi. I hope you can cover the bill."

He twirled my hair, pulling slightly when he didn't like what I said.

"Nice try. This is a shared thing. Fifty-fifty on everything. Unless it is a gift, naturlich."

"I better write home for a bigger allowance." I sat back up. "What time is it?"

"It isn't morning."

"Do we get to sleep?"

"Why?"

"Classes on Monday. I need my brain to be fresh to soak up the international education Mom and Dad are paying for."

He pressed his body against my back and hugged my neck.

"Sleep during the week," he whispered.

"Will you be back next weekend?"

"Oh shit, no. I have a seminar with a French brain surgeon. I forgot."

"Is this how it will be. Me waiting for you to come home?"

"It is a curious thing that trains run both directions." He nibbled my ear.

"Is the seminar in German or French?"

"English in the international lingua franca, mein Schatz."

"Maybe I'll show up," I rested my head against his, in part to stop the nibbling.

"You are assuming I can have guests," he poked my ribs.

"You all but said I could visit." I grabbed his roving hands to hold them tight.

"I will give you my phone number there. You can leave messages with my family. Mutti calls almost every day."

"We will have to figure out how you can contact me. I don't have a phone in my room, and you'd have to warn me when you are going to call the Center. Too many ears there."

"In time, Greyling."

He slipped his fingers along my lips then into my mouth. The taste of sex and sweat lingered on my tongue. A couple of rough hairs coursed the inside of my cheeks. I sucked his fingers until I felt his dick rising against my back. He rested back on the bed and raised me up. I sat on him and rode him until he filled me with his own explosion. I continued to rock up and down until his dick slipped out of me. My musk merged with his sweat. I twisted off to lay by his side. I licked my fingers and circled his nipples with the wet. He shuddered.

At some time in the night, we rearranged so our heads were on their proper pillows. We slept holding each other.

The light of morning brought us around.

Hansi wiped the sleep from his eyes and massaged his beard and jaw. He awakened slowly as I watched.

We did a quick sink wash. He left a note for Leon. He bundled the bedding for washing at home.

We scrunched confidently over the gravel drive out onto the street.

"Hungry?" His first word of the day.

"Thanks. Sure." My weak vocabulary after little sleep. "Where are you taking me?"

"I bought you dinner last night and gave you tickets. Your turn to buy, mein Schatz."

We found a neighborhood café nearby, just before turning onto Neutorstrasse. Tucked behind a hedge, it was not signed as a tourist spot. I bought coffees and continental breakfasts, knowing I'd be visiting the corner store before noon to top up.

We didn't speak much; too tired. We communicated with gesture, eye movement, and flicks of hair. We laughed when we could.

Standing outside his family home, we said goodbye just as my roommate approached. Hansi slipped inside. I turned to greet my friend and went into the Center for a group meeting.

Eight

The clatter of an approaching street cleaner snapped me out of my memories back to my present. More lights on the monuments switched off. The Schloss remained illuminated, always the last to go dark. I turned left to take the long route back.

There must be a back door to his apartment because Hansi sat at the far end of the fountain wall, slouched against the concrete pillar.

"Don't say it," I said.

"Finally learning," he smiled, raised his hand in invitation, and waited for me to join him.

"Thought you were going to bed," I took his hand.

"It is like I am a teenager with you, Greyling. I can't stop thinking of you. I can't sleep."

"Did you try?"

His laugh flowed over the silent water, stilled now from its daily dance. His thumb stroked the top of my hand. I watched the repetitive motion.

"I won't be at dinner on Wednesday if you would prefer not."

"They're your in-laws, for fuck's sake."

"They only invited me after they called to say they had invited you spur of the moment. They were seeking permission and apologizing. Their invite to me was a courtesy."

"Don't be ridiculous. I don't know much about Salieri or Mozart or voice or conducting or anything else related to classical music. In the event of a conversation lapse you will be handy to have around."

He kissed the top of my hand where he had been rubbing the hair off.

"Hansi, inevitable isn't tonight. I am not your sleep aide."

He sniffed and looked up to the Schloss.

"You know, Sam, when the tourists aren't around this town isn't half bad. It is quite beautiful. It took me living in Switzerland to understand that. Being away. Anna Marie moving to Vienna. It changed enough for me to appreciate it."

I replied, "I wonder, if I had come back, whether we would have come to loathe it."

"You mean each other," he looked at me.

"It is possible that our tryst was just a tryst. We would not have survived being a couple."

He looked back toward the Schloss just as the lights stopped.

Even with streetlights, Altstadt fell into darkness.

"I'll walk you home," I said grabbing his hand.

He hugged me. His chin struck my shoulder. I winced but didn't push him away.

He whispered, "Promise me we will be friends."

"At the very least," I squeezed him hard. His smile teased the hair behind my ear.

He unlocked his door. "Are you sure?"

"Waiting for inevitable," I brushed his butt with my hand and walked away. I glanced back. He was leaning against the door frame, backlit by the light from his entry hall. He waved.

"Wednesday," I shouted at the top of my lungs.

"If not before," he dipped his head in a quieter response then disappeared inside.

One side of the street had a series of Konditereis that left decorative product in their windows. Black forest cakes with shiny frosting. Sculpted red velvet cakes with sumptuous decorations. Sacre tortes in Viennese invitation. Licking the window would be frowned upon by the cleaners following me down Getreidegasse and would give scant satisfaction or hints of delicate flavors.

To avoid water splashing my black wingtip-esque shoes, I scampered into one of the passageways that cuts beneath centuries-old buildings. This one was filled with jewelry shops. At the far outer end were the cheaper tourist shops with souvenir tokens. Twisted silver and copper bracelets with matching necklaces. Rings with colored glass in place of emeralds, topaz, and diamonds. I spotted a masculine-weight, pewter-toned friendship ring I decided to check out the next day. Always fun to have a bit of tat that I'll never wear.

Seeing it was safe from the dedicated city workers, I turned back toward Getreidegasse. The sparkle of diamonds convinced me to at least look for something more interesting than a friendship ring.

Most of the rings were engagement in style and baroque in design. Not many options for men, except boring bands of gold, silver, and titanium, which was a craze that didn't go away after it was first introduced. Ugly and emotionless.

In the back row was a line of four modern men's rings each with one discreetly-placed brilliant cut diamond. Gold, white gold, silver, and platinum in similar designs. Enough bling to make a statement but modest in their masculinity. I noted the name of the shop in my phone for further exploration. A dribble of satisfaction coursed slowly through me. I walked the length of Getreidegasse, onto Judengasse, then out to Mozartplatz. I sat in a chair in front of the closed café near the Glockenspiel. The warm evening lulled me. The distant sound of the Salzach entranced me.

The scuff of a pedestrian caught my attention. It was Fred walking passed the sculpture of Mozart in the center of the Platz. He hadn't seen me. As he rounded the corner out of sight, two students raced on the opposite diagonal from Fred's path across the square toward the river.

I sank into a new memory.

Hansi and I traversed the square on our bicycles, racing south intending to climb a mountain on our mechanical steeds as if we were in le Tour de France or a Giro d'Italia stage race to claim the king of the mountain's jersey.

He led the way to the Hellbruner Brücke and across the river. We navigated the small villages along the way with ease but never made it to anything like a mountain. The first hill we encountered broke our enthusiasm, as well as the chain on Hansi's bike, for which a replacement was found in a shop next to a pub where we finished our ride. The return trip was hellish. It turned out that three liters of bier and a couple of brats each don't mix well with a forced ride home. I swore I'd never do it again.

On the way back we lay by the river in some tall grass hidden from the road. People on the other side of the river might have seen us but we didn't care.

With laziness from the warmish day and the remains of drunkenness in his voice, he said, "If we keep trying, we might make it to the top of that mountain over there." His pinky finger indicated a hill not much taller than Kapuzinerberg, lacking the grandeur of le Tour destinations.

"If we keep trying, we might get in shape," I chuckled. "Wait a minute," I continued. "You ski. You hike all over the Alps. Good thing you aren't on the Austrian Olympic team."

"Shame on me." He snuggled closer with his head now on my chest. "You just saw the extent of my skiing and hiking. I get as far as the first refreshment hut and hunker down while everyone else gets sporty."

I rubbed his sweating back. He moaned his pleasure.

"Come to dinner tomorrow," he said out of nowhere.

I choked and that got me coughing so we both sat up. "What?" I asked between gulps for air.

"You can walk me to the train station after."

I was still processing his suggestion because two weeks after our first tete-e-sex I wasn't sure I was ready to meet the family. "How are you so comfortable with this?"

"Are you worried about them knowing something? Greyling, I told you, they know and are fine. They will make fun of us but that's their way. Anna Marie thinks you're a dream and will change your mind for her."

"Your Mom and Dad?"

"Mutti's brother was killed by the Nazis. Vatti is so laid back he's practically dead too. They are fine. They want to know if you are as smart as I tell them."

"Am I?"

"My very own Einstein. Say yes. If you are uncomfortable or boring, we won't invite you again anyway."

"I'll be a burden." I crossed my arms on my knees.

"An Austrian Hausfrau cooks for double the number of place settings. Vatti will eat what you don't. It's the same simple meal every week. Beef roast. Pork sausages. Roast potatoes. Fried vegetables. Sauerkraut. A minced compote of pine nuts and berries. Ending with Strudel. All homemade. Oh, wine for the meal. Bier for after."

I gulped, "Except for the sausages, kraut, compote, strudel, wine and bier, it sounds like home."

He slipped his arm between my torso and my legs resting his elbow against my groin. His pumping elbow got the dick reaction he was after.

"Did you talk to Leon about this evening?" My head tipped back. I screeched my frustration.

He looked at me while pumping away. "That is the first unpredictable thing you have said this weekend." He stopped and pulled his arm out. "Interuptus maximus, nichtwahr?" His laugh startled ducks waddling next to the river. His stopping startled me.

"We have to find Leon," I said, pushing him away.

"His little brother is visiting."

"He can take the kid camping!"

The exasperated ducks flicked their wings and dove into the Salzach.

"Let's go tell Mutti you are coming to dinner." He pulled me up. "Walking or riding?" He looked down at my bulge. "Walking then riding, ja."

An hour later he parked his bike against their house; I parked mine at the Center.

I hesitated.

"Come on," he motioned. "The worst that could happen is that she'd bake you for dinner."

Frau Adelheid Wortmann was the sweetest Austrian Hausfrau I would ever meet. She wrapped me in a hug that went on for days. Her breasts massaged me as she twisted me with delight. Her large hands held my head against her neck. I couldn't see Hansi to try to give a silent scream for an escape. She also spoke flawless English into my squelched ear.

"My American son has finally come to us for dinner. You must come every week. You are the son I always wanted. You make me so happy."

Five minutes later, my back was aching. The strap of her apron imprinted into my cheek. Her swept back hair fell over me so my introduction to Austrian welcomes got hotter and hotter.

"Mutti, halt," Hansi said.

Relief poured out of me like the perspiration wiggling down my chest. I plastered a good old American smile on my face to confirm my own delight at freedom.

"Sam will only come when I am in town and maybe not even then. He has commitments with his student group. He has to study, too, don't you Sam?"

Now the tether ball of family politics was in my court. I didn't have a clue what the protocol was. I stuttered.

"For instance, Frau Wortmann—"

She interrupted but Hansi stepped in to block any further maternal assault.

"You will call me, Adelheid, mein Amerikanischer Sohn."

I nodded assent, glancing toward Hansi who had turned to pour a glass of water from the iced pitcher on the kitchen counter.

"Yes. OK, yes. Indeed, Adelheid, Frau Wortmann."

"Mutti, your new son is slow to make up his mind. Patience will be rewarded." He winked either at her or at me. "You were going to say, Sam? Something about studying in a foreign country?"

"Yes. Well. For instance, next weekend our group is going to Munich for Saturday and Sunday."

"Oktoberfest? Wunderbar. It is so much fun. Perhaps we could also go and meet you there. Ernst said he didn't want to go this year. He would wait until our own little harvest celebrations in Salzburg. Those are fun as well. You will join. That is all settled."

"It would be awkward, Frau—Adelheid. We are training up and back both days. And—"

Hansi was being no help.

"Mutti, don't be surprised if he brings you a souvenir gift from Munich." He nodded in my direction with his subtle hint.

I retorted, "I am sure that with Hans' help I will find the perfect gift." I didn't divert my stare from his glowing, smiling face. "Perhaps your son can escort me to my studies today." I reached out for Adelheid's hand, thinking I would proffer a very English peck. That was not to be. Again, I was engulfed in Austrian hospitality.

Hansi tapped me on the shoulder. "Let's go, Sam. Mutti, let him go."

We walked past the Center and beyond the corner store.

"She likes you," he said when we crossed Leopoldskronstrasse.

"She doesn't know me. What about your father?"

"He's a church mouse. He likes that his children are happy."

"How is it that in this world they are so welcoming. In America it is still dangerous to be open. I won't know what to do when I go back." I tried to laugh but the reality grabbed my heart.

"Don't go back," he said as nonchalantly as breathing.

"Wouldn't that be nice," I said. "Living in a film for the rest of my life. Are you coming with me to my room?"

"You need a shower," he pushed me into the street. "Do all Americans sweat like you?"

"You aren't exactly a field of flowers." I jumped onto the sidewalk to avoid a bicyclist who was clattering his bell like a freight train.

"We are going to the sport gymnasium," he declared.

"I thought we settled that sport isn't our thing."

"They have showers."

"I'm not a member."

"They also have a steam room. Saturdays there'll be no one there."

"I'll shower at our lodgings."

"Greyling, you are so dense."

"It's empowering. You should try it," I said, bouncing ahead of him like the scared rabbit I was emulating. I knew what he was angling for. It was not a question of density. The discomfort nudged me into rodent mode. Not the horny kind. In two weeks, I had been pushed so far out of my comfort zone I was all but peeing my pants.

"We'll shower then sit in the steam room. Nothing needs to happen unless you want it. You let me know what you want to do."

"Am I a prude?" I settled back into step next to him.

"The jury's out." There was not an ounce of humor there.

Shit, shit, shit, I thought. I am a prude. Jesus Christ on a crutch. Loosening up was proving challenging.

"OK. Shower and steam."

He slouched his arm around my neck and pulled me to his chest to the point that I almost fell.

"You are such a momma's boy, Hansi," I said, pushing off his hip.

"Don't ever insult my mother." His laugh echoed through Maxglan.

It was odd to me that one was to shower before a steam room where one would sweat, but that's what we did. Lots of soap-dropping and laughter in the tiled echo chamber. He grabbed my hand pulling me to the farthest reaches of fog. I couldn't see two feet in front of me, but he found the corner seating with ease. I suspected he'd done this before. Ain't no prude, that one.

He maneuvered me to the top row of seats and wasted no time. He was down on me like a rabbit. He slipped his hand over my sweaty body to my mouth and clasped me shut. I held on tight even as the door to the steaming boudoir of sport opened and two voices entered. Hansi withdrew from my dick to cough. Yup, he's done this before.

I peered through the wafting fog. Between gulps of excitement at the pumping of my dick, I listened for where the two voices landed. Hansi's masterful silent sucking gave the other guests no reason to suspect a thing. My cough was too high-pitched though and Hansi cuffed the side of my face. It wasn't a slap but a warning for silence. I was figuring out how I was going to cum stealthily, which is not my forte.

Hansi controlled that too, by slowing down, extending the excitement and the danger. He eased jizz out of me instead of demanding an explosion. It felt like an elongated pee after a four or five liter night at Augies. He grabbed my legs with one arm and held them so I wouldn't stamp my feet or thrash about.

His other hand still on my mouth allowed my ecstasy to recede in fits and starts. His tongue milked me dry.

Sweat poured out of me. Our end of the fog was wetter than wherever the other men sat, silent, listening, relaxing in their own special way.

Hansi crawled up next to me. His hand rested on my thigh and I leaned back until my breathing was steady. He leaned over to my ear and whispered in small releases of air that didn't disturb the fog, "You are a god. Thank you."

Before I could say anything, he said out loud, "Time to hit the showers."

We rinsed quickly then sat at a table with our towels between our asses and the wooden benches.

"How did you do that?" I marveled.

"Practice, Greyling. Something you and I need more of."

Nine

The striking of the midnight hour returned me to Mozartplatz. I didn't know the Glockenspiel played all night. A few drunken tourists tried to sing a drinking song but they fell flat both in tune and walking. Then Fred entered the Platz, retracing his steps from his crossing minutes before.

I watched him pass behind the Mozart sculpture and then look up, catching my eye. I returned his wave.

It was time to get to my hotel. I made to stand, but strong hands grasped my shoulders and pushed me down. I panicked as Fred laughed.

"Unlucky at love, Herr Greyling?" He struggled to pull a chair away from the chained table.

"You're a busy man tonight," I said, ignoring what I thought was an insult and then realizing it was his youthful humor.

"Had to get this from a friend," he brandished a thick tome in front of my face as if it were too dark or too foggy for me to see, even with two safety lights glaring across the Platz.

"When do you go to Munich?" I asked.

"That was cancelled. Voice instructor came down with something."

"What's the book?"

"Cervantes."

"Which one?"

"You know Cervantes?"

"Americans know how to read," I said.

"You have so many great writers. You don't need to read this old stuff."

"Old stuff is referred to as 'the Classics'." I cringed my air quotes.

"Like you, Sam," he flirted.

"It was fun, Fred, but not tonight," I insisted.

"The great American holiday in sleepy Salzburg wearing you out?"

I laughed, "Something like that." I stood to leave.

"I'll walk you back."

"Don't you have a classic to read?"

"Around the corner, Sam."

We walked in silence and arrived at the street level door.

"I'm a big boy, Fred. I can do the rest by myself."

He hesitated a second then kissed me on the cheek. I wanted to push him away, rebuff his advance, parry his thrust, get away as fast as I could.

I awoke alone in my bed. A glance at the clock let me know I was late, even for a lazy tourist, and had missed my free breakfast. 10:31 a.m. I rolled back to the center of the bed and moaned.

"What's the matter, old man?"

Fred's voice startled me into sitting and swinging a pillow in front of me for defense. He raised his book in salute. "Cervantes," he chortled. "I may be your Sancho, Herr Greyling."

"I truly hope not, Fred." I threw the pillow in his direction, although it didn't make it past the half-on duvet. The dishevel of the room reminded me why I remained so tired. "I need to sleep. You need to go."

"Sam, don't be like that. We had fun. It will come back to you when you have your coffee. I can order room service."

I ran my fingers through my hair and slapped both cheeks. "A shower will help." I slid off the bed.

"I've been waiting." He stood, naked as the empty bottle of scotch on the floor. It had been a full bottle, which meant I'd ordered room service.

"Room service won't be able to get in the door. I'll go out. Housekeeping will be knocking soon. Out you go." I threw his jeans and sleek, button-down shirt further than I'd managed the pillow. I looked for undergarments that might fit his upper body bulges and his tiny little waist. I realized he arrived with two articles of clothing sans belt but with some sort of Austrian flagged, masculine espadrille. Not into footwear they might have been deck shoes. I didn't care. I wanted him out.

"You are such a prude," he said.

"I've heard that all my life," I replied as stern as an old, naked, American Quixotesque knock-off rather than a horny homo able to perform all night could reply.

"Don't you have a recital to do or a play to perform or a dance number to fuck around with?"

"I like you, Sam. I want to hang with you. Prudes are attractive in a repressed way. Although, Sam, I must say, you were not prudish last night. That first blow job was amazing."

"First?"

"You must teach me that move," he walked toward me, sword ready for the next windmill to come along.

"Shower. Then you leave."

"Prude."

At 1:00 p.m. housekeeping knocked on the door. The phone rang at the same time.

"You should unplug your phone," Fred said, dragging his arm across my chest and rolling to the other side of the bed.

"I've heard that all my life, too."

It was nearly 3:00 p.m. when we emerged into afternoon light and a mid-week tourist frenzy.

"Why don't you move to Vienna?" I said, approaching the river and the bouncy footbridge. "And why are you a barman?"

"I didn't fuck your brains out, did I? I'm a student at the Mozarteum. Come to Vienna with me. I have a recital in two weeks."

"I'll be back in America by then," I said, working hard to be disinterested.

"You are retired. It's a three-hour train ride. Expenses paid. I am sure they will include a guest if I ask. Some friends will be there. They will love you, Sam. Please stay. They'll buy you single malts the whole time."

"I'll think about it," I said, trying to avoid a commitment. "I have a life back home."

We walked for longer than I needed or wanted to. "I don't want to walk too much further for my next meal. You have an idea?"

"It's a bit prissy but you'll like it. My friend's sister's mother-in-law owns it. Used to be an old fag bar back in the day."

His nonchalance insulted my hallowed memories and I stopped in my tracks. He crossed the street unaware that I was not following.

"Come on," he waived me across, "it's not far. End of Steingasse."

On his side of the street, I said, "I know where you mean. Not for me."

"It's decent food and a good laugh. Might get a free glass of wine."

"Fred. Let's head down river. Keep it simple."

Roiling through my skull were the memories of Hansi, my youth, my awakening, the year of terrific turmoil that chased me away then brought me back. I couldn't mix Fred into those memories. That was the insult. A visceral repulsion. I needed to keep Hansi of the past separate from anything in the present. For my still naïve brain this was a major problem. I was struggling to hold Hansi different from what I sought today.

"There's a Wurstl shop not far. Will that be enough?"

"For now."

"Will you tell me what's going on?"

"You are too young to understand."

"Sam. Insult is beneath you."

"I wish people would stop telling me what is or isn't me. I came back to find myself and all I find is what other people want." The child in me wanted to throw a tantrum.

Fred started past me. I stopped him.

"It was a fun night, Fred," I said.

"You don't remember most of it," he shot back.

"Still," I turned sheepish. "Let's skip lunch. I want some time alone."

"You need to eat. Come on."

"What are you doing for breakfast tomorrow?" I took control.

"Practicing the Lieder for Vienna. Margarette is in town. Our soprano. I have booked a pianist. We won't finish until after midday. Sam, please tell me what is going on."

"I don't know." I have got to stop this lying.

"I want you to come to Vienna. Please. You have become important to me."

"After a few nights of sex? Fred, don't patronize."

"You know there is more."

"No, I don't know. I told you. I don't know."

I walked up the incline to Steingasse. I didn't look back because looking back keeps getting me into trouble. My resolute stride got me halfway up Kapuzinerberg in no time. I sat looking over the city I love—a city holding too many pressures. Cell service up here was lousy at best.

Fuck.

I thought only of escape. Paying the $500 air penalty. Getting back home to some sanity. Reconnecting with friends I had lost or shunned or tolerated. The agony of Thomas overwhelmed me. I shouted the irony of "Haben noch einen schönen Tag" to whatever human, deer, gay man, or city that was listening. I scrunched onto the bench and cried the pressure, fear, lies, and agony out of every pore of my being. I didn't care anymore. What did it matter anyway. I was going home to a mediocre life in a mediocre city with mediocre friends. Not-my-first-love Thomas stuttered in my head. Staggered through memories. Raged in his unique jealous way. Decades of tension from two lovers poured out of me. One lover held the fantasy of perfected youth. One lover held stability, companionship, excellent sex, and the jail of mediocrity. One lover gone to death and haunting. One lover inviting me back.

Then there was Fred. An echo of youth abandoned. Better in some ways because his body was near perfection. His sex, both the act of and the organ, was absolute perfection. Plus, he was smart, interesting, talented, focused, engaging, flattering, and all together an option for an older man.

Drying my eyes and blowing my nose, I saw myself walking through Vienna with a boy toy on my arm, adoring his every move, supporting his every choice, laughing at his youthful—meaning not mature—jokes. While I didn't doubt he could introduce me to people my age, I knew the gossip and whispers would tear at us, would poison his hopes, would describe everything he would be missing as a twenty-something Wunderkind, because he was clearly talented.

I lifted my head off my arm lounged over the back of the bench. Smacking my forehead woke me, got me out of my funk of self-sorrow.

"That bastard," I said to all of nature. "What a fucker." Trees shuddered from a healthy breeze flowing north out of the river valley. It cooled the air but didn't come close to cooling my anger.

I grabbed my phone. No bars. Shit. Shit. Shit.

The pity party ended.

On Linzergasse I poked my head into a taxi. "Do you know where Gunther Drecker lives?" My sweetest American gay voice tinged with self-deprecation.

"Everyone in town knows," he said, in a gay voice not tinged with self-deprecation.

"Double the euros if you get me there as fast as you can,"

I trusted I wouldn't be taken for a ride because I had no clue where we were going except that Hansi had said he lived in a mansion outside of town.

"Wait for me. This will only take a minute," I said, exiting the cab and leaving the door wide open. He pulled forward out of view of the main entrance.

The boy who answered the door was the same blond, skinny thing that Gunther licked a few nights before.

"Get Gunther now," I said in my lawyer voice that I hoped was a global phenomenon.

"Is he expecting you," the painted toy said.

"Waiting for me, yes."

"Please come in," he stepped aside.

"No, Herr Drecker comes here."

Lawyer worked for now. He scampered away, leaving the door ajar, possibly breaking every rule of the household. Dispensable boy toy.

The trundle of Gunther's sandaled feet echoed in the marbled foyer. The door glided open from behind revealing the man himself standing in a yellow, orange, and beige kaftan. Every color I avoided like an infestation of rats.

"The honor is all mine," he said, waving his toy away. A tiny rat dog barked in the distant inners of this Rococo, moderne mashup.

At least the ambiance encouraged my resolve to attack.

"The privilege is yours, indeed," I spat back.

"Sam, you must come in to cool off."

"One question. Do you know Fred Gluck?"

He shuffled forward one step pretending to be thinking, something I doubted he did much. But what do I know.

"Who is this Fred?"

"Answer the question," I retorted. My lawyer voice not having an effect.

"Oh," he placed his index finger against his lips and turned his head to the side. Pose. "Is he the Fred who sloshes alcohol in that bar off the Steingasse?"

I turned to leave with my answer tucked somewhere in my brain.

"He is so delicious and so very talented. I understand you know this. His delicious talent."

I tried not to stop in my tracks. The top step was a doozy. I caught myself before tripping down the other five. I turned on my heals.

"Do you have any clue how disgusting you are?"

"One man's disgust is another man's lust, I have found." He placed both hands on his breasted chest.

"Doesn't change the fact that you disgust me."

"Fred takes my money and my attention. His lust is gratifying. Stimulating on quiet nights by the pool. You should join us. Every Wednesday in good weather. I'll send a car. Does 9:00 p.m. work?"

I crunched across the circular drive noticing the statue of Saint Sebastian emoting in the center surrounded by a cupola featuring Rococo angels with bows pointing more arrows into the youth's body. The driver spat gravel toward the still open front door. Gunther waved goodbye. His sardonic smile disgusted me more.

I didn't know the address of where I wanted to go. My description got me close to Fred's bar. I threw €100 into the front seat and opened the door.

"Card only," he said. That might be why the back of the seat was covered in six languages yelling 'card only' at any fare brave enough to enter. I took the cash back then told him to add €60 to the exorbitant fare on his card reader. I accepted that hazard pay was a valid charge.

Fred was sitting on a skinny, carbon-dated stone bench attached to the bar.

"Have you eaten?" I skimmed his coif with my hand and kept walking, turning south on Steingasse.

"Wait. Slow down," he shouted, once he realized what had happened.

We arrived at my old pub while five pant-suited ladies in striped, off-white linens stepped gingerly to street level in their heels. We waited, not offering hands for support. They tittered their afternoon wine buzz.

We were seated at a two-top on the balcony railing, and ordered sandwiches, pommes frites, and Oregon white wines in honor of home.

Fred waited. Sensible, since I was now contradicting myself in an old Quixotic way.

"I need to tell you something. Then I need to ask you a question."

He nodded in silence. Intelligent youth is beguiling.

I told him the history of this place that will always be a pub to me. I told him about my youth in Salzburg. I didn't tell him specifically about Hansi or that I knew Gunther, but got close enough that if he knew Hans, he'd reveal that on his face or in posture shifts.

Sandwich, frites, and wine came and went. He listened, still. Engaged youth is intriguing.

"Now for my question. Your answer is key so take your time."

I ordered more wine.

"Verstehen," he said, scratching his head.

I waited for the wine. Fred waited for me.

I squared my body and leaned in.

"What would it take for you to abandon Gunther?"

"Gunther?"

"Ja, your bank. That Gunther. The one I knew years ago and don't care to know now."

Confusion cascaded from his forehead to his mouth, pausing for a microsecond at his eyes. He scratched his chin, fingering the slight cleft that anchored his film star looks.

"You know him." He deflated. Perhaps regret. Maybe relief.

"I understand," I sympathized. "He's an old man. He's got something you need. You want to get somewhere. I'm not judging, just observing."

"He came to me. He saw me. He heard me sing."

"He flattered you until you were knee deep in his lust."

"I didn't see another way. My family can't help. The bar is great but with rent and everything else I was short when it came to lessons and travel."

He sat back in his chair. His hands flat on the table he raised his shoulders in consternation and near defeat.

"The minute I can, I will drop him," he said, relaxing back into a slouch.

"What would it take?" I repeated. "Don't be shy."

"Sam, I—"

"If you want to achieve what you want you must do it without Gunther. He sucks life from whatever he touches. You've seen it happen. I see the fear in you."

He rubbed his forehead.

"Pretend he isn't in your life. What would it take?"

"It isn't the money, Sam. Well, it is. It's just—."

I waited.

"He said he'd ruin me. In an instant. I have to go there after work tonight. Now I am afraid what he will say." His pleading tore through my heart. Talent crushed by the power of one man.

"There's no time to waste, Fred."

"What can you do?"

"I don't know but if I don't have a target, I can't move, let alone help."

He gave me a number. Monthly. In euros, so I had to convert. Then I doubled his modest amount knowing that youth don't understand the cost of living. I thought about ways to save, to cut back, to make it work. I settled on a plan.

"I have a request," I said, paying the bill.

I waited for the server to bounce down the stairs to street level and into my cubbyhole. I pushed nostalgia into its proper grave so I could focus.

"Don't fall in love with me."

Fred drained his wine glass and then drained mine.

"Find someone your age. Have an affair. Don't tie yourself to one person. You deserve everything you want. A younger person can enjoy that with you for much longer."

He leaned forward.

"Did you fall in love with Gunther back then?"

I brayed and another wine patron shushed me. Fred stayed sullen.

"Not Gunther. The other one I told you about."

"He's why you came back?"

"Not specifically. Possibly. Probably. Yes, OK, yes. I came back for him."

He grasped my hands in his.

"Then I have competition."

I pulled back.

"No competition. That is settled. I know what I need and want. Part of that is to help you get what you want."

"I want you, Sam."

"I'm not available, Fred," I said with absolute certainty. "I would apologize to you, but I have enjoyed our adventure. It is time for both of us to move on."

I stood. He sat back. I offered my hand. He waved me off. I walked down the stairs then waited on Steingasse for him to join me.

He clumped onto the cobbles.

Before he could say anything, I said, "Come with me tonight. A small dinner party. I'll cover your wages if you take the night off."

"I'll still have to go to Gunther's."

"If you still want to after dinner."

We stopped in the middle of the footbridge. He leaned his back against the rail and I rested my forearms to watch the flow of milky blue water.

"I should walk away from you, Sam. My body wants to run because of the pain you are causing me."

I slouched sideways and rested my hand on his arm.

"I am flattered that you feel the way you do, Fred. It wouldn't work. You know that. Honesty now makes it easier tomorrow and the next day. Besides, I think tonight, if it all works out, will help."

He turned to look down at the fast-flowing river.

"In these few days I have learned to trust you." Fred said. "You are the only person who has captured me this way."

I pushed my shoulder into his.

"We'll be friends. That I know to be true."

He snorted derision.

I continued. "When I first met you at the bar, I saw you as a hot fuck. You are a hot fuck. I have learned with you that beauty is not skin deep. Cervantes, for fuck's sake. Knowing American literature. Being interested in an old fart like me. You remind me of my first adventure here. Fresh off the boat. Driven to learn and explore. Fearful of too many things. By the way, you are fearless. Or will be once you get rid of Gunther. I hope tonight changes everything for you. I know it will for me."

"Do you always babble on endlessly, Herr Greyling?" He smiled for the first time since before lunch.

I touched his cheek.

"The world will know your beauty," I whispered.

He shrugged me off. "OK." His mature resolve forming. "I'm gonna trust you. Once. If tonight fails me, I will not be your lover or your friend. Are you ready for that?"

"Incentive to get it right," I smiled.

We lingered.

He kissed me on the cheek. "Please don't make that our last kiss."

"Meet me at the foot of Linzergasse at 6:30. Dress to impress but don't overdo it."

He walked back the way we came. I watched him enter his bar and leave less than a minute later turning onto Steingasse and out of sight.

I had to find Hansi to work on a few details, including how to tell our hosts that there would be a couple more for dinner.

Ten

We arrived at the Steiners' at exactly 7:00 p.m. Hansi was already there.

I apologized for intruding with my plans for the evening. I introduced Frederic Gluck. We both offered appropriate cheek pecks. Hansi shook Fred's hand.

Herr Steiner said, "You only need to apologize once, Herr Greyling. Five times must be an American mannerism."

I apologized again, prompting laughter—and yawning motions from Hansi.

After being seated, and waiting for the proffered pre-dinner beverage, Fred leaned over and said, "How do you know these people? They are very famous in Austria."

"All to be revealed, my friend," I said.

Hansi watched from his corner chair, soaking it all in, and waiting for the main course.

Herr and Frau Steiner served a killer Gewürtztraminer. I suspected Hansi hosted beverages, but then given the art and antiques I was ogling, the Steiners might have a wine cellar with varietals from their performing travels.

"We have so much to learn," said Frau Steiner, sitting on the settee, wine glass in one hand and the other placed lovingly on Herr Steiner's thigh. The tableau said everything about years of respect, honor, and devotion. I looked at Hansi and smiled.

There was a silence I broke unspectacularly, "I was sorry to hear about Andreas."

"Why?" Herr Steiner asked, inured and calmly. "You didn't know him."

"Hans has spoken of him. I cannot imagine—." I looked at Hansi for help because once again Austrian social protocols failed me.

"We are told you can imagine," Herr Steiner said unperturbed. "Hans tells us your own partner died a few years ago as well. Is that not true?" He looked to Hansi for direction. Hansi remained detached.

"Yes—Thomas—died three years ago. It was a difficult time."

Frau Steiner said, "Losing loved ones so young is a tragedy, Herr Greyling. We all have something in common then. Unless Herr Gluck has been more fortunate." She looked to include Fred who looked like a deer in headlights.

"My family is alive and well. I am sorry for your losses," he said. He lowered his eyes probably wishing he was at the bar pouring cocktails for errant gay tourists.

"Much to celebrate," Frau Steiner raised her glass in a toast.

"Indeed, there is," said Hansi from his perch. "So much to learn tonight." He looked at me, urging me to tell why Fred was at a party as the guest of a guest, something he hated for his own parties, so this had to be driving him insane. Except that he knew the plan, so I shot him a look.

He turned to his in-laws, "What have you for supper this evening? You usually have surprises and delights."

"Nothing terribly special, Hans," Herr Steiner said. His chubby cheeks turned red. His grin broadened. "We hope you will enjoy it."

The double doors to the dining room opened. A smartly dressed caterer said, "Supper is served."

Fred hit my leg with his hand. "Awesome," he whispered in English.

The Steiners led the way. Fred followed. Hansi put his hand on the small of my back and pushed me forward.

"This better go well, mein Schatz, because they don't take kindly to rude intrusions on their lives. As you can see, they have reputations to protect. They survive on that."

I stopped him before we passed into the dining room.

"Then I would appreciate your help. Fred is not a threat. Have a little patience. Some encouragement from you would be much appreciated."

I turned to sit between Frau Steiner and Hansi with Fred across from me.

A smoked fish on goat cheese amuse-bouche with a Tirolian bread greeted us, paired with a new white wine. That was followed by a Speckknödelsuppe, delicate and complementary, wine topped up as needed. The main course was a Chateaubriand that melted in the mouth. A red wine was introduced. A light, refreshing green salad followed.

During the meal was when I had hoped to present my plan to the Steiners and to add some detail for Hansi. I trusted he would understand why I'd withheld these details when I first spoke to him. The meal was so intriguing and the wine so varied that we ended up talking foodie until we were invited back to the lounge for dessert. Herr Steiner requested a twenty-minute respite but "please serve the after-supper wine".

Back in his highchair and with everyone relaxed and sated, Hansi said, "Sam, I believe you have something to discuss with Mutti and Vatti?" It was the first time he had used the familial endearment, signaling to be kind and do not insult his loved ones.

"Right. Yes."

All eyes turned.

I presented my plan with each item followed by my reasoning and cost estimates. Costs as in money, time, and personal engagement. I avoided the word sacrifice because I was convinced none of this was going to be a burden.

I turned to Hansi, who was deep in thought, looking at his Vatti and Mutti in-laws to gauge their responses.

"Hans, there is a part of this I didn't tell you earlier."

"Why am I not surprised, Sam," he said, weary and wary.

"What I have presented so far is a way to help Fred become a successful performer. I am certain the plan will work." I turned to reassure the Steiners.

"I am also suggesting that you move back into your family home and Fred move into your Getreidegasse apartment—with roommates. They would pay rent but not at market value. They would also be musicians on the rise, in training, preparing for the world stage."

Fred jumped in, more out of embarrassment, "I have an apartment."

"Paid for by Gunther Drecker," I shot back.

Herr Steiner coughed. "Is that Drecker fellow involved in your plan, Herr Greyling?"

"He's involved in controlling people's lives and careers." I was a bit too strident, but that truth was now out.

"Your plan is about thwarting Drecker?" Herr Steiner said.

"It is about recognizing that talent is being wasted for his ego, which means extracting young people like Fred from his grip and supporting them in achieving their goals."

Steiner looked at his wife. Her sadness melted her face into a frown of despair. She turned to me. "That man has been the bane of the arts community in Salzburg. He has weaseled onto boards and thrown money around to gain notoriety. He is dangerous, Sam. You must understand that you are crossing a narcissist who will stop at nothing."

It was obvious they had fought the Drecker juggernaut. My naïve illusions of philanthropy fell away. I turned to Hansi who paused before speaking because the dessert tray arrived followed by a shot of schnapps for each of us. We took our time savoring the Sacre Torte and raspberry liqueur.

"Mutti," Hansi said, "Would you be able to sing this evening?"

"Yes, Hans," she said with a skeptical twinkle.

"Vatti, how are your fingers?"

Herr Steiner stood and took his wife's arm. They led us into the music room.

"Wow," Fred said, turning to take in the shelves of sheets and books of music and cupboards filled with vinyl recordings. Herr Steiner sat at the baby grand piano in the middle of the room. I noticed the stunning royal Kashqai rug beneath it.

He launched into the introduction to a Lied. Frau Steiner sat next to him on the bench. Her coloratura entered on time. Thirty seconds later, Fred stepped next to the piano. He waited for a cue from Herr Steiner. On time, his tenor slid under her soprano. Their voices intertwined. His virile tones complemented her softness. She stood and walked to Fred, who stepped away from the piano to hold her hands. Their duet lightened their faces. They merged into near perfection.

When the song ended and the piano rested, Herr Steiner said, "We will do this. We will help Frederic Gluck and others as best we can. It must be done, Katarin."

"Without delay, Anton. Hans, what must be done?" Years shed from her.

Back in the lounge, Hansi outlined his thinking.

"I'll talk to Anders this weekend. He'll know a good attorney."

"Who is Anders?" I asked.

"Sam, sometimes I wonder how you stay so smart. He's Andreas' brother. He's Anna Marie's partner. In Vienna. Mutti and Vatti's last son." His chumped-up face asked if I understood. I chumped back that I did.

To the Steiners, he said, "I'll keep you informed as we go along. Basically, we'll create a trust to protect your assets. We'll add three-quarters of my assets so they are protected, including Getreidegasse and Neutor. That will shield us from anything Gunther tries."

I chimed in, "We'll add the same amount of my assets, as well. That should create a good fund for young artists."

"Sam, that is not necessary." Hansi said. "Our assets should be sufficient. It's not cheap to live in America. This isn't a competition."

Fred leaned forward, "Wait, Herr Wortmann. Sam? What are you saying?"

I looked from Fred to Hansi. I could feel all four of them staring at me.

"I am moving to Salzburg," I said. "I'll extend my stay for two weeks, alert my real estate agent of the pending sale of my home, I'll go back and put everything in storage, and come back to see this through. I can work with my banks and financial people to liquidate my assets from here."

"Slow down." Hansi said.

"It's a done decision, Hansi."

"Maybe you can handle the American end of things," he said. "Where will you live? What about visas? There are details."

Herr Steiner interrupted our domestic interaction, "We know people who deal with visas all the time. We'll call in the morning. You have ninety days as a tourist then we'll need to worry."

"There, see," I snarked at Hansi, "there's always a way."

Fred set his schnapps glass on the table and stood, "What happens to me. Gunther will go after me to spite you two."

Hansi put his hand on my shoulder, "We'll move you in with me tonight. Then I can figure out what to do with my tenants."

"He'll make sure I don't have access to teachers and pianists, even in Munich and Vienna." Fred sat and put his hands on his head. "I need to go to that party tonight. He'll know something is happening if I don't."

Frau Steiner stood to clear the dessert dishes. "Anton, help me, please."

Anton smiled and did as he was told.

Hansi said, "Fred, we will go to the party with you. Maybe arrive at different times. You interact with Gunther as you normally would. Sam and I will run interference. Added benefit, we can see what other musicians might fit into our scheme."

I thanked Hansi by touching his hand, which he squeezed to give ascent to my plan.

"This will work, Fred. Three of us can outwit that dimwit," I said.

Herr and Frau Steiner appeared at the double doors. The server followed holding a silver tray with five digestifs. She distributed them then said she was done for the night and looked forward to helping in the future.

We sipped our cognacs in thought.

Herr Steiner leaned forward, looking at Frau Steiner who nodded encouragement.

"We would like to offer a solution of sorts," he said solemnly. "Frederic will stay with us. We will be his voice and piano teachers. In return, he will help us with small things like grocery shopping, cleaning, and other chores. He can stay in Anders' old room. We will figure out the rest as we go." He nodded with conviction.

Fred looked at Hansi.

"That is most generous," said Hansi, "but it is also a burden. The three of us will figure out what to do. Your generosity tonight has helped immeasurably."

"Hans," Frau Steiner set her cognac down, "you are missing one piece. Herr Greyling needs a place to stay. He cannot be renting a flat in Salzburg. Out of the question. It is logical he stay with you and Frederic lives with us. If Frederic agrees, of course."

I added my two cents, "I'm not sure living with Hans is a good idea."

"Why not," she said, "You love each other and have for years. Andreas knew it. We know it now." She turned to Hansi. "Andreas loved you, Hans. He also carried a sadness that he was not your only love. It was merely sadness. If it was anything else, he would have left. That devotion will never die. Now that we know Sam better, we understand your long dilemma. We see now that you held two loves in one heart. We love you, Hans, like our son. In time, perhaps we will love Sam and Frederic as sons, too. It is our decision to offer this solution." She put her hand on Anton's thigh. "You would be fools to not accept." She downed her cognac. "Now it is time for bed."

That was us told. We stood as a unit. The new family we'd become.

Herr Steiner added, "Fred may move in tomorrow. We will be ready." They turned to go. "Let yourselves out," he dismissed us with the backward wave of the hand I first saw on Kapuzinerberg a few days before.

Fred gathered the digestif glasses and took them to the kitchen. Starting his new duties immediately.

"That went well," I smiled at Hansi and grabbed his shoulder.

He shrugged me off.

"Not to linger. We have a party to attend."

"What is this?" I said, holding him from bolting to the door.

"You blindsided me. You are so predictable," he huffed.

"Apparently not too predictable because you didn't see it coming, mein Schatz."

He touched my cheek. "I am going to fuck you so hard you will think we are both twenty years old."

"Inevitable," I grinned.

Eleven

Fred arrived by bicycle. We arrived by taxi. We sent him into the swamp of the Hydra fifteen minutes before us. It was nearly midnight.

The host was lounging on a chaise throne on a dais facing the lighted pool. Colors of the rainbow shimmered in the splashing water.

"Your party was lovely, Hans," Gunther said as we approached. "I apologize for crashing it so completely. Larger party; smaller crash for you, darling." He extended his hand. We didn't bother.

"Quite the Roman ruin, Gunther," Hansi said.

"Indeed, the boys will ruin me, nicht wahr," he winked my direction for approval or a laugh or an acknowledgement. I still didn't bother. "Outdoors in summer, we include the ladies. In winter, indoors is more intimate. Men only. Join in. The pool is yours. The boys are yours. The ladies are yours if you wish to explore beyond your usual comfort."

We pulled a couple of chairs from the pool deck to the dais forcing the toys on either side to shift. Gunther flicked them away.

"How do you do it, Gunter? Get all the best people at your parties?" Hansi jumped right in. I might have waited.

"It's a talent," he said, licking his fingers for no reason.

"Where are the older Salzburgers?" I queried.

"Home in bed, I would think," he parried. "Can I get you a cocktail? Single malts? Two fingers, I believe. Your friend Frederic is so valuable."

"How so?" I feared our Fred was playing both sides but couldn't make eye contact with Hansi to show my concern.

"I can flip a tourist faster than you two can sneeze," he chortled. "Eyes and ears. It's a way to fundraise, you know. Horny American tourists with wives and families back at the hotel. Wanting a night alone. Friends like Georg are helpful, of course."

I wanted to rip into him about blackmail and people's reputations and the immorality of his enterprise. I was startled to see Hansi rip off his shirt, shoes, trousers, and underwear then dive into the pool. He came up next to a dark young man, probably Balkan or Turkish. But what do I know.

Gunther laughed. "Still has his lovely body. You are so lucky, Sam." He lolled his head in my direction and smirked.

"Ah well," I said. "I return to America next week."

"You'll be back."

"You know, Gunther, I probably won't be. I got what I wanted this trip. There are other sites to see."

"We have time to go to Venice," he sat up, rearranging his dayglo kaftan for modesty and to hide his flab. "Before you go. I can arrange for you to fly from there, so we have more time."

"I'll take that single malt, if the offer stands," I said.

He sent a minion to the bar for two drinks and two plates of canapes. He made sure to insert the descriptor 'French' before the barely legal boy scurried off as directed.

Hansi monitored the situation while he splashed with the younger set who took to him like orca to whales. Good thing he still had his body because he would have drowned if not. Tired and sucking air he crawled up the ladder to plop into the chair.

"So invasive," Gunther tried to escape the shaking of hair and squeegeeing of body that rained chlorinated wet onto him and his throne. "So rude of you, Hans!"

A boy brought a towel and offered to personally dry Hansi. Hansi let him, turning toward Gunther as he held the boy's hands drying his genitals in a rotating fashion. The boy looked trapped in old man hell. Gunther wanted to look but turned away in false modesty, shielding his eyes. Hansi laughed loud enough that some of the guests turned to see what was happening and themselves broke into laughter.

Hansi dismissed the boy and finished the job himself, throwing the wet towel behind the chaise. He sat down again just as the drinks and canapes arrived.

Gunther leaned off the chaise in my direction. "Your pal Frederic is at the other end."

"Didn't notice," I lied, with no remorse.

"He seems to be enjoying himself with Toby and Lynda. You remember them from the recital, I think?"

"Ah, yeah. So he is. You know, Gunther, I'd get bored doing this every week. Same pretty bodies. Same immature knowledge of the world. Don't you get bored?"

"The world bores me, Sam. We used to talk about that way back in the Middle Ages."

"If you recall, *you* talked. I listened. That was your way, was it not? Non-stop? To avoid boredom."

"Depended on the company." He motioned for a boy to approach. "A plate of melon." He sent him off with a twist of his wrist. "You were easy to enthrall. The American waif soaking it all in, never questioning, always eager. Much like these—." He swept his arm over his subjects. "Now, with the means to do so, I am lord of my dominion."

"And bored," I said.

"Content," he lied.

The melon plate arrived.

Hansi stepped in. "I have never understood what you do for these kids. What happens to their careers in the arts?"

"I offer a refuge from the stress of their lives."

"Do they simply leave? I guess Americans and Canadians and Japanese go home and build what they can from what they have learned. I'm not clear how it all works."

"Every one of these youths," he motioned like he was counting them one at a time, "lives in an apartment I provide. Every single one has tutors I pay. Each of them has lessons as many days of the week as they want. I manage them. That is how it works."

"Don't most of them get scholarships or have support back home?"

"That's a trifle of what they need. Most of them get to the Mozarteum with nothing. I merely assist them."

I stood and stripped off my clothes.

"Oh," Gunther whined, "another mature body. How truly lovely."

"Why don't you join me for a paddle," I said, turning full frontal toward him.

"Can't stand being wet."

I ran to the pool and did my best cannonball, which at my current weight was mediocre at best. Enough to backsplash onto the dais. When I surfaced, Gunther was recoiling and calling for boys to come dry his chaise. Not happy.

I swam to where Fred was talking with three men and a woman.

"Anything?" I asked, turning him toward me.

The five of them ganged up on me and started drowning me. Between dunkings, Fred told me he had a dozen who wanted to talk to us. They were all disgusted but felt trapped. As expected, the discontented were older and later in their schooling.

"Stop. Enough," I spluttered, escaping to the side of the pool for a rest. Dedication to the plan. I calculated the cost of a dozen or more. Doubt surfaced. I hung tight to the pool until my breath was normal and then crawled out and walked the deck, assuming none of the young folk were watching.

Gunther and Hansi were watching.

As I approached, Gunther broke into applause, "Your death-defying skills eclipse those of Herr Wortmann, Sam. I am impressed with how you interact with my friends."

I yanked the towel out of the hands of the dry-boy and avoided wet falling on Gunther or his chaise or his kaftan. He settled down and asked the boy for a glass of French wine.

"That wore me out," I said, pulling my clothes back on. "Time for me to go. Thank you for a rewarding evening, Gunther." I turned to leave and then feigned an afterthought. "Out of curiosity, how many students do you support? It must be rewarding to help when you can."

"How many can you count?"

"They are all here?" I did a quick tally. Thirty-five. Not counting the boy toys, bartenders, food runners, and clearly hired staff.

"Oh, indeed," he sparkled. "Missing one of my parties has consequences, gentlemen." He turned to Hansi, still sitting naked in the chair nursing his single malt. "Are you staying the night? It would be enthralling if you would."

I rolled my eyes, "How many do you figure?" I didn't let it drop.

"I sponsor twenty each year. Would you like the car to take you to your hotel? I assume that is where you are going at this late hour?"

"I think I'll walk. I count twenty-five in and around."

"It's nearly five kilometers, Sam. Your swim must have tired you." He motioned for one of the boys to tell the driver. "At this hour. I want you to survive until tomorrow at the very least."

"I'll be fine."

Hansi had still not moved to dress. His legs were spread and his dick dangled. "I'll see you later, then." I tried to catch Hansi's eyes as I dethroned.

Gunther said after me, "Your count is correct. I am screening my youth for next year."

I took a page out of Herr Steiner's book and waved him away as I walked out.

Out on the drive, the skinny blond toy boy opened the door to the host car.

"I'm walking. Thanks." I leaned down to say goodnight to the driver. When I stood, Rheinhardt drove up in his mini car, too small for his long torso. I waved and kept walking. He drove around the tortured St. Sebastian and pulled up next to me, driving at my walking pace.

"Leaving early, Herr Greyling?"

"Leaving on time. Have fun in there."

"I'll drive you."

"A walk will do me good. Too much bier and wurst."

"You don't want to do that at this hour. Salzburg has an underbelly you don't want to confront."

"It's a few miles. What could happen?"

We continued down the long drive toward the road that wound its way into town. I was confident I could find my way, avoiding turns down uninviting roads.

Rheinhardt pulled in front of me to block my way. "Don't be stubborn. Get in. You'll be in bed in ten minutes or less."

He convinced me. I climbed in and scrunched my body into the seat.

He found a parking space near the river.

"I'll walk you back. Nefarious people could jump you." The wry smile told me he might be the one jumping.

"Don't assume anything by this."

"After seeing you at the party the other night, I don't assume anything." Wry turned to charm.

It was late enough that I had to ring the bell for the night manager to let me in.

"Thanks, Rheinhardt. You don't want Herr Drecker displeased with you." I waved him away. He stayed, leaning against the building. I rang the bell again wondering if the manager had fallen asleep or was stuck in the toilet.

I'm still not sure how it happened but Rheinhardt ended up in my room. I wondered if Gunther taught his minions the art of stealth manipulation. He was an expert. No one learned those skills by osmosis. Rheinhardt seemed a quality pupil.

I waited for him to pee. I had weakened when he begged me to use the toilet. I stood with feet firmly in place, firm against the flattery and flirting. We both knew what he wanted. I knew what I didn't want. Then again, he also avoided the toilet in the lobby. What did I know.

He left his trousers unzipped and unbelted. His shirt was three-quarters unbuttoned. So much for the flirt and the flattery. Get to the point, Rheinhardt.

"No," I said, "No. You go, now."

"Dad worked my ass off today," he said, wriggling his firm butt like a dog needing a fuck.

Before I could counter, he opened the minibar and grabbed a bier. He tossed me a mini bottle of scotch. "Bottoms up," he smiled. His trousers slipped to the floor.

"You're paying for these," I said.

"I plan to," he opened his shirt, sat, and removed his shoes and trousers. His underwear had dinosaurs scattered on them.

Fuck. Fuck. Fuck.

I laughed at my choice of thought bubble. He thought I was laughing at his choice of undies.

"They make me happy." He stood; a couple of dinosaurs closer to me than the rest of his body.

"It could be worse." I intended that for internal consumption but there it was out in the space of my hotel room, which was turned down and had two Mozartkugeln pressed into the pillow so they wouldn't roll away.

"It won't be better." His confidence continued to grow.

What did I know.

The next morning, I knew. I woke up exhausted with two Mozartkugeln crushed beneath me. Rheinhardt gone.

"Getting too old for this."

Missed breakfast again. I calculated how many morning meals I had paid for and thought about what I could do with that money instead. I vowed to wake up earlier, and to slow my libido, especially for these young men who for some reason wanted sex with an older man. So many beautiful Austrian men and available tourists but they fuck with me. I'm good with that and curious at the same time.

I tossed the chocolates in the trash bin.

A knock at the door.

Shit.

Through the door peeper, I saw Hansi staring at the little hole.

"I see you," he lilted like I was a child playing peek-a-boo with him.

In my nakedness, I opened the door and walked back into the bathroom. He followed, leaning against the doorjamb as I peed.

"Disheveled. Black rings under the eyes. Smashed chocolate on the bed sheets. Your hair spiked in more directions than exist on a compass. I wonder who you were up to after you left."

"You don't look like you've even slept, old man."

"Lots to tell, mein Schatz."

I pointed at the shower and then my body.

"Great!" He was too enthusiastic.

"What? No, Hansi." I threw him a towel and closed the door behind him.

"Inevitable, Greyling," he shouted through the door and streaming water.

After he dried off in the bedroom, doing dance moves I had never seen before but smiling all the while, he said, "Last night was fun."

"How so?" My attempt at boredom made him laugh. Happy to be of service in the humor department.

"I hung around long enough to learn what goes on with all those young bodies and alcohol and other stimulants. He spikes the punch. Viagra comes out in bowls. In the morning his toys drop more chlorine into the pool. He should drain it and start over."

"In the morning?" I brushed my hair one more time.

"You left at one. The ladies left at two or thereabouts. Then the party started. I couldn't leave. There was too much research to do."

"What are you high on?"

"I didn't drink the punch if that's what you are implying."

"Comforting. You hungry?

"Exhausted is what I am." He hugged me from behind with his chin on my shoulder.

I looked at his tired eyes in the mirror. "No punch but morning Viagra?"

He huffed his delight in my ear. "I think inevitable is ending soon."

"I think you need to eat then go to bed for twenty-four hours. You were the oldest there." I shot a smile his way and wriggled out of his grasp.

"We know part of how he keeps them attached."

"We know the whole picture. Money. Money. Money. Delivered in different ways. The question is how we break their addiction to it."

"According to Toby and Lynda, your fat stalker also dictates what they can perform. He sets their schedules, plans their travel, chooses their play lists. He controls them by threatening loss of support."

I threw his clothes at him, even though I was enjoying the revival of disco fever.

After practically dressing him myself and worrying that he had imbibed the punch that must have been spiked with speed, we got to my usual breakfast joint. I walked him to his recovery nest in Getreidegasse and said I'd collect him for dinner at six, and reminded him we had to act quickly to help Fred.

As I turned away, bumping into a tourist with too much bling dangling from every limb, I said, "Vienna calling!"

He winced. "I'll call Anna Marie right now with apologies. You'll come next week, right?"

"Go to bed, old man. Where is Fred?"

Fred was packing.

"I am embarrassed," he said, as I grabbed a bag and stuffed his shirts into it. I invited him to say more by staying quiet.

"I saw so clearly what Gunther is up to. It was hard to not walk out. I knew I had to stay until we have the plan in place. What can I do to help?"

"Hans has to do his bit. I suspect that will be delayed a day or two."

Fred chuckled, "It's been great getting to know both of you." His hips circled and thrusted telling me one result of Hansi's research.

"I didn't realize he was a big old slut," I laughed.

"Unlike yourself, *Herr* Greyling." His emphasis on Herr made his point, along with three quick thrusts in my direction.

"I hope you aren't going along with this for sex, Fred. It is serious stuff. If you are going to use us, go back to Herr Drecker and let's stop now."

"I would not screw the Steiners. They will help me more than anything Gunther can do."

"If you screw the Steiners, we will screw your career more than Gunther will try to do. Capiche?"

He sat in a little folding chair in the corner of his little studio apartment. I reminded myself that youth will adjust to any living environment, something I would no longer do.

"I fear my career is screwed no matter what." Pain and fear were etched on his face and eked out through his tenor whine. "Sometimes I think you are doing this to get revenge. That you care less about me and more about winning some decades-long battle."

"The truth?" I said, sitting on the single bed.

"You did say this was all about the truth." his tone shifted downward to a light baritone.

"He haunted me when I lived here as a student, much like he is controlling all of you. He knew I was back in Salzburg before I knew I was back in Salzburg. Not revenge. Release. Freedom from a controlling freak."

"He isn't all bad, Sam."

"Are you sure? The intensity of his control is so much greater than when we were young. He has changed. In a bad way. That is why we are doing this, Fred. Not out of revenge or because we don't like the guy but because you are better than him. You have the talent and skills he craved but wouldn't do the work to achieve it for himself. He's buying what he couldn't have."

"He has an empire."

"Not enough for him. One would think wealth, and the power that brings, would be enough. He needs youth and energy to hold it together. Our enterprise is small compared to him. Our aim is more noble."

He continued packing.

"Fred," I grabbed his arm to stop him, "I knew we were right when Frau Steiner stood from the piano bench and sang with you. The ethereal look on her face astonished me. It must have been how she looked in her youth. You have your own power, my friend. You will not realize that staying with Gunther."

I looked around the room.

"Leave the stuff in the kitchen. You won't need it where you are going."

We hefted his stuff across town. Herr Steiner welcomed us. Frau Steiner was tidying Fred's new room.

They waved our thank yous away to get right to the point.

"What Lieder are you preparing for the Vienna recital? Where is the recital? Who else is performing? Have they printed your selections? What criteria did you use for your Lied selections?" They meant business.

Herr Steiner and I schlepped Fred's stuff to his room and I stayed there to unpack. Fifteen minutes later, as I pushed the last antique drawer closed, the piano started up and voice-warming exercises began.

Before I let myself out, I shook Herr Steiner's hand and waved a kiss at Frau Steiner. I didn't disturb the happiness that permeated Fred. I knew we'd made the right decision.

Now for the hard part.

Twelve

Neither of us would be partying all night any time soon.

I crawled up Hansi's stairwell holding on to the banister, the walls, the stairs in front of me. He waited at the top with a firm grasp on the landing banister. We sat in the living room, him with head in hands and me lounging against the sofa.

"You must call Anders to see what he can do. It can't wait until next week," I said through meshed hands in front of my face.

"Did Fred get moved?"

"Had his first lesson with the in-laws fifteen minutes after I moved him in."

"One safe," he moaned.

"Get some food in you." I pulled him to his feet. "Let me see if you pass for a tourist so we don't have to go far." All he needed was flip-flops. "Still in your party costume. Tsk-tsk. A respectable tourist would at least have a button-down Hawaiian shirt untucked to show his emerging vacation belly. Come to the bedroom. You have anything like that, Hansi honey?"

It slipped out. I hadn't called him that since two or three weeks before I'd left the last time. I let it hang in the stale air.

"While you change, I'm going to open the windows. Refresh the air."

"I need a shower," he said.

"You do. The one this morning didn't get all the party sweat. You do have a distinct orgy odor about you."

He stripped off. "It wasn't an orgy."

"A Fred orgy then—."

"It is good to share."

"He can do what he wants."

He climbed into the shower tub, humming a disco anthem, stopping the exchange from turning ugly.

"Where do you want to eat?" I said from the living room. I heard him travelling from drawer to drawer and pushing hangers aside in great heaps. I feared Europe was not equipped for my wardrobe.

He emerged in linen shirt and trousers with grey belt and sandals. His hair perfect. Face glowing. The inevitable was getting closer. Once again, practicalities overrode inevitable. Hunger smacked it in the face.

We emerged from the tunnel into Neutor.

"Will this work?" We stopped in front of a Greek restaurant.

"Perfect. We can take the Augies route back to Altstadt," I said in a tired chuckle.

"Nothing like more alcohol to overcome a party night." He pushed me through the gate and up the steps.

Waiting for our small meal in the back garden, he said, "I spoke to Anders and Anna Marie. He can get a basic trust set up quickly. The slowdown will be the government paperwork. He said filing the paperwork shows intent. He thinks that offers a foundational layer of legal protection.

Appetizers arrived while I pondered.

"Fred needs one of us near until his recital," I said.

"You want to fuck Fred." His tone was brutal.

"Jealousy is a wasted emotion, Hansi. Unbecoming and rude." I softened my response. "I can visit your mom. I will be at the recital in case Gunther plans to disrupt it. And I'll meet Anna Marie and Anders."

"I thought this Trust was a partnership," he dropped his attack mode.

"It is, or will be once it is in place."

"Until then it's business as normal?"

"Hansi, what is going on? If this is going to work, we have to figure this out."

"You are doing this to spite Gunther."

That hurt. I sat back, listening to the clatter of the kitchen and the traffic just over the wall.

He reached to take another spanakopita.

I grabbed his hand and held it tight. "Let go of who I was. Meet me here and now."

His blue eyes watered. "I thought I was." His head dropped but he tightened his grip. "It is no secret that I want you in my life. That I want you in Salzburg. I also know you might not want that. Once again, I feel like I am grieving your passing."

"I told you in front of witnesses that I am moving to Salzburg. What more can I say?"

"Am I to believe you? When you go back you might change your mind. You did before."

"Let me change, Hansi. After Fred's recital I'll go back and do what needs doing. Thirty days, then I'll be back."

"I want to trust you—." He pushed the spanakopita into his mouth.

I couldn't tell if the water in his eyes was because it was too big a bite or fear that he couldn't trust me. I had to show him and not merely request he come along for the ride.

Luscious, cool Greek salads arrived. Full of color and taste. It calmed me when it was set in front of me. The interplay of the complexity of flavors presented the truth that I needed to compromise if any of this was to work. Moving to Salzburg with a major mess on my hands would not be productive.

"Hansi." Tentative. "I'm fine meeting Anna Marie and seeing your Mutti. We can get things set up with Herr and Frau Steiner. Help Fred not freak out. We can make it work."

"If he focuses on his training and doesn't go out, he'll be fine."

I must have sighed too loudly.

"What?"

"It's not about Fred. It's us, Hansi. The Trust Fund and helping these kids is secondary." I opened my hands in frustration.

"I'm agreeing with you, Greyling. Take a break, for crying out loud."

Maybe a change of direction would help.

"We need to name this trust fund. Anders will need that, I would think."

A second bottle of wine arrived.

"One way to neutralize Gunther, is to not use our names at the top. We can also honor someone else," he said.

"I've been thinking that the Anton and Katarin Steiner Trust has a ring to it," I parried.

"I was thinking the Andreas Steiner and Thomas McCormack Memorial Fund," he chimed or charmed.

"Nice," I pondered with wine glass to lips. "What if we did this: Steiner Trust, then two funds within the trust named for Thomas and Andreas?'

The server removed our plates and presented the dessert menus. Hansi pulled out his phone.

"That's perfect, Greyling. I'll text Anders. I also like that structure. One fund can focus on classical performing arts. The other on what? Modern performing arts?"

"Maybe there needs to be a third fund that is general to encourage exploration in the arts, digital, and support performance events."

"We can work out the details on the train."

"The Hans Wortmann," he slashed the air, "slash, Samuel Greyling Fund for Arts and Performance."

"No. No. No." I wagged my finger. "Alphabetical. Samuel Scott Greyling and Hans Stepan Wortmann etc. etc. etc." I raised my glass to toast the solutions, and more importantly, the compromises.

My baklava tasted sweeter. His revani went down with a moan of contentment.

We walked by Augies with no intention of stopping. Both sleep-deprived, we needed to get some stuff done prior to the upcoming frenzy and my departure.

Fred opened the door to the Steiners' apartment with an alpine grin, teeth for miles.

"This is so fantastic," he said.

"Are you going to invite us in?" We stood on the outer stoop enjoying his enthusiasm.

Herr Steiner arrived to pull Fred back and open the door wide. His smile was more relaxed, if somewhat tired. He looked happy.

"I've poured your single malts, no ice," he said inviting us to sit. "Katarin will be out in a minute. She's got something for you."

I was hoping for cake.

Fred fidgeted.

"You're wound up," said Hansi.

"I have learned more about my voice in two days than I have in years. Anton and Katarin are the best. Thank you for making me do this."

"It was your decision," I said.

Frau Steiner entered with two large envelopes in hand. She, too, appeared tired but still glowing with pride.

"Hans, you must take these to the people and addresses on the outside. You must hand deliver them. As soon as you can tomorrow you must do this. It is critical to the plan that you succeed. Am I being clear on how urgent this is?"

"What are they?"

"Don't open them under any circumstance. They must not be compromised. Do you understand, Hans?"

"You can tell us what they are, Mutti," Hansi said.

"Frederic will be the talk of Vienna. His voice is ethereal. His love of music is grounded in knowledge. The critics will respond well, I think. Don't you think so, too, Anton?"

"Without doubt, Schatzi," Anton deferred.

"OK. We'll deliver them tomorrow."

"Fred. You aren't at the bar," I said.

Fred agitated more.

"I quit," he said with confidence. "It was in the way of practice. Too many distractions. He looked over the top of his glass of juice.

Herr Steiner jumped in, "He understands that to become a professional he has to stop as many distractions as possible. Working late and sleeping late sap the energy." He dared either of us to disagree.

"I can also pick up another class in music theory," he puffed with pride.

"He is very good. He can be better," Herr Steiner said.

"You will make him into a conductor then?" Hansi asked.

Frau Steiner sat between Hansi and me. "He will be able to make better choices for his voice," she said, indicating it was her idea.

Herr Steiner said, his cognac poised in front of him, "Your friend Herr Drecker stopped by at midday today."

"It's starting already," Hansi croaked. "Tell us."

"Nothing to tell. We didn't let him in. Fred told him to go away."

Frau Steiner tittered.

"I told him to go fuck himself," Fred crowed.

I shot a look of concern over the top of my glass. I recovered enough. "Was he alone?"

"Despots always have enablers hanging about them," Frau Steiner said. "He got in his car and yelled at the driver. Do not worry," she patted the envelopes in Hani's lap, "these will take care of that problem."

"What mischief are you up to," Hansi touched her hand.

"Andreas would be proud. He 'worked for government', you know." Her air quotes highlighted her seriousness. Her manner of delivery made us laugh, except for Fred who wasn't in on the history of Andreas' career.

"We'll know soon enough," Hansi side-hugged Frau Steiner.

It was nearing dark when we left. Pleased. Too tired to talk.

Hansi walked me back to the hotel.

At the door he said, "Check out early and bring your things to the apartment. We can sort it out as we go."

"Are you sure you want this, Hansi?"

"You're staying in the guest room. We gotta save money now."

He wet my lips with his luscious tongue then walked away. After he turned the corner I got to my room, packed, and set the alarm. I didn't want a wakeup call because I didn't want Georg knowing my plans. My check out goal was before he arrived and before Hansi's suggested time. I can be stealth when I want to be.

Thirteen

Our first task after breakfast was to deliver Mutti Steiner's envelopes intact and unopened. We hoofed it to just off the Linzergasse to a small alley with a hidden door—uneasy to find. We left, not filled with confidence, but the elderly gentleman who accepted our delivery through the barely opened door assured us Frau Steiner would be happy with the results and the delivery would be made on time. Delivery of what, we weren't entirely sure.

The second stop was a PR firm of note because they proudly displayed a ten-kilometer-long list of clients spanning all of Austria, southern Germany, and lands beyond. We were starting to form an idea of what Mutti Steiner was up to but accepted that we would only know for sure on the day.

Hailing a cab for the ride to Mutti Wortmann's home, I said, "Thank you for doing this." I wasn't sure what I was thanking him for, yet it was heartfelt.

In the cab, he covered my hand with his. "Mutti will be pleased to see you."

"Hansi, I cannot express the sorrow I feel for abandoning you. There are no excuses for my actions, or inactions, I suppose."

He lifted my chin so he could look at me, the way he melted my heart so many times.

"I have enjoyed our wrangle these two weeks. Seeing you at Augie's that first day was a shock. I followed you to confirm it was you. I was rude. We got off to a bad start."

I leaned into the palm of his hand. He stroked my cheek with his thumb. Eyes locked in soppy pools of joy and honor and whatever love we were mustering.

"Besides," he said, "if you hadn't stayed away, we wouldn't know the Steiners and have our stories to tell."

"There's that," I said, looking at the rolling alpine foothills.

Castle Wortmann, as Hansi called it, was nestled into the tree-covered hillside. It was more Romanesque villa from northern Italy than fortress protectant. The Dorian colonnaded drive was deceptively short because the columns decreased in height. Red and yellow floral strips filled the space between columns. Low ferns and bracken created an illusion of sumptuous lawns. The circular drive surrounded another floral display that surrounded a plinth that supported a three-foot-tall Dorian colonnette topped with a modernish sculpture of the Virgin and Child.

"Andreas hated that sculpture. He wanted to leave money in his will to pay for a replacement. The facility's board turned him down. He plotted to steal this one in the dead of night to replace it with one he felt was more appropriate. His replacement idea was just as ugly."

I pondered the statue as I took in the view back toward Salzburg and the Untersberg in the distance.

"Beautiful," I thought I whispered.

"Your taste in art scares me, mein Schatz." An arm around my shoulder.

"The view, is what I meant. That," I pointed at the drooping virgin about to drop her load, meaning the child and her load, "is—I agree with Andreas. We should melt it down and start over."

"Let's do that," he kissed my cheek.

I didn't have time to laugh out loud because the foyer of this elder nursery was nearly as large as the nave of one of the churches in the heart of Altstadt. While Romanesque in architecture it was filled with incongruous cupids, clouds, saints, angels, and who knew what else all in a Baroque gaudiness that insulted the senses. After an audible exhalation of my shock, I did laugh out loud.

"Even Mutti says it's over the top."

"That's one response," I replied.

"What are you going to do when you convert a monastery."

He pushed his shoulder into mine.

Before I could respond, he shuffled off in the gait of someone three decades older. Fearing I'd be lost in what was clearly a maze of corridors leading away from this artistic horror I loped after, my laugh awakening the cherubim and seraphim from their stony frieze.

Hansi rapped lightly on the door with the same number as the street number of their home on Neutorstrasse.

We waited.

He rapped again.

The shuffle of feet on wood floors approached, accompanied by a dainty cough.

"Kommt gleich," said the wispy croak.

We waited for the door to open.

"Hans, meiner Sohn," she said. "Komme, komme."

"I come with gifts," he smiled.

"Viel spas." Her smile drifted into the hall. I imagined her looking at his empty arms in consternation and confusion.

His laugh rattled up and down the corridor.

"Eins mehr für Midtagessen," he said, as his hand shot out and grabbed my upper arm; my biceps and triceps ached before he pulled.

I lurched into the doorway.

"Wer ist das?" she squinted. "Ach, mein Gott."

She flew like an Austrian eagle to engulf me in the familiar hug, which had softened in intensity but was as heartfelt as every time before.

"I told Hans you would return." She raised up to kiss my neck. "Mein Gott. Mein Amerikanischer Sohn." She withdrew her hug and covered her mouth with both hands. Tears shone in her clouding eyes. She hugged me again.

"Mutti," said Hansi. "May we come in?"

It was a single bedroom apartment with a small, built-in kitchen unit that was too efficient for words, and a functional bathroom with walk-in shower and one of those fancy baths that the user sits in while warm water fills around them. There was an ample terrace large enough for a few chairs, a four-seat dining table, and pots for plants fit for the jungles of Peru, that I surmised were tended by the gardeners I could see weeding flower beds on the other side of the English lawn.

I took all this in as Frau Wortmann engulfed me in another hug that I had missed for too many years.

"Mutti, you are still strong enough to crush him. Let him go so we can talk."

She pushed me back but didn't let go.

"Shame on you, Sam. You broke our hearts. Why did you not come back?"

Tears shone to near falling. She daubed a hanky.

"He's here now, Mutti. Sit down. There is much to catch up on."

"I am most happy to be back, Frau Wortmann."

"Sam, you are not to call me that."

"Adelheid—," I corrected myself with a smile as warm as I felt.

"You have not changed, my son," she said dropping heavily into a chintz wingback chair—a throne for a dignified queen. "I want to hear all about your life now. Your life without us." Her stern glance was a reminder of how she ruled the roost wherever she went.

"Mutti," Hansi said, "that will take days. We will visit more before he goes back to America."

"You are leaving again?" Her glare darkened.

Hansi stepped in. "He's going back in a couple of weeks." He raised his hand to stop me from promising I would be returning. His admonition to not disappoint her should my plans fall by the wayside struck at my core.

He continued. "In the meantime, we will take you for lunch and drives to the Salzkammergut if you like. And we will take you to Vienna soon. There is a concert recital by a new singer. We think you will like him. Anton and Katarin will join us. We will go by train so you can sleep if you want."

She patted her knees.

She turned to me. "Sam, I want to know about your life without us."

I filled her in on the basics of my life, leaving out Thomas for now but playing up my career so she could feel good about one lawyer replacing another in Hansi's life.

She gushed about Anna Marie and her music. She enthused about Anders but avoided mention of Andreas.

Her photo album escaped its hiding place fifteen minutes into our visit. Hansi took this time to clean the kitchen, bathroom and bedroom, then folded some clothes and put them away. He might be of use yet, I kept thinking as I watched him out of the corner of my eyes between motherly slaps to my leg to pay attention.

"Mutti," he said as the last bureau drawer closed with a thud, "it's time for lunch. Did you tell them you would be out?"

"Oh." She flustered her hands to her hair. "I forgot. Will they be mad at me, again?"

"They won't be mad, Mutti, because they will still bill you for the meal. Not to worry. I'll phone them now."

She closed the album kissing the cover photo of her husband and squeezing the book to her bosom. Her coy smile added cheer to our memories.

We decided it was easier to dine with Mutti Wortmann's acquaintances at the home. We sat among the elderly being eyed by the women and scrutinized by the men. Our brazen laughter at Adelheid's memories garnered enough tsk tsks to last a lifetime.

Back in her room, Hansi tucked her woven blanket around her. She settled in for her afternoon nap.

"We'll be back soon to prepare for Vienna and for Sam to tell you stories."

After hailing the shitting virgin, our first stop was the Steiners to see how Fred was faring, and that Vatti and Mutti were holding up. Second stop was the apartment to rearrange the living quarters. Third stop was Augie's for a light supper, which is an oxymoron at a biergarten, and strategizing next steps.

Fourth stop was a walk through Neutor and Maxglan, passing by the original Castle Wortmann, the Center, and places of first contact a couple of weeks prior and many years before. We plodded up Monchsberg to sit and watch the lights come on. The bench we used to sit on had been replaced by a stone and slate overlook with multiple benches and tables. We sat looking away from the tourists in a bubble of 'us'.

"Are we doing the right thing?" My ability to ask multiple questions in one was rooted in my parents' fear of scarcity after the upheaval of the mid-century gone before. Or I was very clever. What did I know.

Hansi leaned against me. The lights of the Glockenspiel popped on as it played 8:00 p.m.

"You did that on purpose," I chuckled, twisting to kiss his head.

"Coincidence is not causation, mein Schatz," he said. A small amount of tiredness slipped behind his smile.

"Do *you* think we are doing the right thing?" he followed up.

"You did that on purpose, too. Not answering by asking." I sat forward forcing him to unpark his head. "I'm not falling for that gambit again."

"OK, then. The manner of your asking tells me that you think we are doing the right thing. How's that for a direct answer."

I pushed my knee into his. "Circuitous at best, Schatzi." I smiled at having picked up Herr Steiner's endearment for his wife. It was a one-off use and pushing a boundary for me.

He covered for my awkwardness. "For Fred, we are doing the right thing. I'm saying that not as his one-night stand fan but because Mutti and Vatti Steiner are convinced he is talented."

"Concur," I needlessly inserted.

"The rest of it I am more tentative about. Too many questions before we can implement it. In that time, your pal Gunter could disrupt the plan, destroy Fred, and ruin Mutti and Vatti's reputation." He paused overly long. "Greyling, I don't know if we can pull it off."

I inserted helpfully, "We can't launch until we have the legal stuff in place. We play it like a one-off, focused on Fred. We counter anything your very good friend Gunther throws at us. That way we learn his tricks before we launch the Trust."

"Holy crap, Herr Greyling, you actually are an attorney."

The lights across the river, on Kollegienkirche, Franziskonerkirche, St. Peter's church, and the Dom, danced on one after the other. The glow and shimmer of lights on water indicated the fountains had all been turned on. We waited for the big one.

"I think we wait for the Trust until after I return," I said in anticipation.

Hansi grabbed my hands and held them in a tight ball.

"I'm coming back, Hansi."

The lights of Hohensalzburg flashed on, throwing blues and greens and whites from end to end.

We cheered better than any tourists behind us. We shared a kiss for luck, as one does in these moments. We basked in the lights illuminating our world.

"I feel like a Wiener Schnitzel," I said with the gusto of a mountain dweller.

"Being caught up in the moment does not lead to good culinary choices, mein Schatz."

"A heavy meal it is!" I struggled to extricate myself from the table and chairs.

"Wine with bier chaser it is!" He tangled up the same way I did.

When the lift deposited us at street level, we abandoned Schnitzel to climb the stairs to his flat.

"Two fingers?" He read my mind.

I stood at the window looking at the tourists on the square below. My drink was delivered by two arms encircling me, one glass without ice for me, the other with, for him. He rested his chin on my shoulder and I leaned my head against his.

It had been decades since I'd allowed his love to engulf me so thoroughly. If I were a cat, I would have purred. Perhaps I did because he chuckled and unwrapped himself from me to sit in his reading chair. I continued to peruse the view.

"I'm not sure why I am nervous about this," he offered, apparently to test something.

"It will work out," I replied.

"I will be devastated if it doesn't."

I shot him a disapproving look. "Gunter will devastate you only if you let him."

"You, mein Schatz. I'm talking about you." He did that thing with his finger, inserting it between his lips. He was too deep in thought for my liking.

"What's the worst that could happen? I die in a plane crash." I laughed. He moaned.

We remained nervous though. The inevitable was nerve-wracking.

"Mutti Wortmann seems content," I said.

"You are not to call her that." His laughter rattled his library.

"I never liked calling her Adelheid. She's your mother."

"Andreas never warmed to it either but with Frau Wortmann you do as you are told."

He chugged his remaining single malt. I nursed mine.

"Do you miss him?" I asked.

"Every second of every hour of every day. Etcetera into the universe."

"Can you share him with me?"

"No. What I can do is show you what he taught me, what he did to make me a better man, how he impacted me. He is mine to remember. Yours to enjoy through me."

He joined me on the couch, resting his head on my shoulder.

"You seem more vulnerable than I remember you, mein Herz." I was pleased to discover my own endearment. He snuggled closer. "You were the strong one back then."

"I let someone love me." He ran his hand along my thigh. "I could not have done that without you first."

"Don't over credit me. I would feel responsible."

"You should. It's OK to be responsible for someone. That's a foundation for love."

"Hail, Saint-Exupéry!" I toasted with my single finger of scotch.

"A bit Alpkäse, yet apropos."

"Cheesy, indeed."

His smile rustled through us.

"Do you remember I read that to you?"

"Yes. In French. Muddling my brain while I was working on my German."

"You can't muddle what is already mucky."

I pushed him away to sit on the edge of the couch.

"You also read me Hesse. Enlightenment through insight. First forays into game theory as metaphor for life."

"This is no game, Greyling." His shadow crept back.

I swirled my liquor in the warming glass.

"Thomas taught me that life is a form of play," I said. "Agreed rules of engagement allow for spontaneity within the confines of those boundaries."

I stood, intending to engage more scotch.

He rose also, to engulf me in another hug. Wortmanns were huggers. I would need to loosen up. But talking about spontaneity killed spontaneity. I shut my trap, anticipating the inevitable.

I disengaged his embrace to remove the glasses from our hands. Health and safety is a good rule.

We cuddled.

"I am sorry that I missed you so much," he whispered into my chest.

"Perhaps in time we will both be released from sorrow," I posited into whatever universe of play we inhabited.

"Are there goals in your play theory?"

"Play as if your life depends on it. It's not about winning and losing; it's about playing honestly and completely."

"No holding back?"

"Inevitable."

He maneuvered me out of the living room, leading me by the hand as if for the first time.

He slowly unbuttoned my shirt and lowered it from my body. He kissed my neck. His tongue wet my chest then encircled my nipples. Ripples of glee coursed through me. I exhaled my excitement. He raised my arms and licked my pits. His expertise evident in how he dropped my trousers before I could lick my lips in anticipation.

Thank you, Andreas, I thought lasciviously, wondering who taught whom the wiles of masculine sex.

I stepped from my trousers then raised his face to mine. I taught him a Thomas move of the tongue eliciting a moan of satisfaction. I felt his excitement in his trousers as I repeated his unbuttoning and loosening and dropping, finding myself on my knees in front of his older man undies and his sword of distinction ready to engage.

Shorts down, I had his dick in my mouth stroking him the way he had taught me. He shuddered. He groaned.

His still firm ass responded to my massaging and spreading. I searched for his hole and fingered him while I sucked him faster. His gut and leg muscles tightened as if he were about to dance his anticipation. I pulled away and stood. He moaned against me but recovered quickly to push me onto the bed. We scrunched our way into place. He had my shorts off before my head found the pillow. Relaxing into the coarse duvet cover I heard the nightstand drawer open and close. Not wasting time with intimate foreplay, he had me akilter and opened in no time.

"I will never hurt you," he said as he penetrated me hard and fast.

"Do it," I whispered after the first four thrusts of his huge cock. I released memories to be in this moment of play time, recalling the rules we had set long ago.

Hansi rode me while I grabbed his ass and made him do it hard and fast.

As he shot into the condom, he fell on me then thrust his tongue deep into my mouth. We kissed and writhed, hands exploring bodies we had never forgotten. I found the muscles on his back I always stroked when we kissed. He found the spots on my neck and throat that drove me to ecstasy.

He gently took my balls in his mouth and rolled them side to side. He gagged as he had done our first time and came up for air with a laugh of remembrance. Before either of us could laugh more he devoured my dick. His stroke familiar yet new. My back arched as I came. He sucked every drop from me until I shuddered and begged him to stop.

He crawled through the disheveled duvet to snuggle into my side.

"Inevitable," he gasped, more out of breath than the last time we had fucked.

"Thank you," I whispered through his hair.

"I love you, Greyling."

It hung in the air.

His eyelashes fluttered against my neck.

"I love you, mein Herz," I said into the universe.

Fourteen

The six of us disembarked at Wiener Westbahnhof.

Mutti Wortmann went down for a nap in her own room. Fred, with Mutti und Vatti Steiner, cabbed to the new venue because she had—stealthily and through the help of her extended network—moved Fred's recital to a larger space, one she felt was a better fit for the occasion. It also sent a message to Gunther that we were not to be trifled with. We saw them return through the lobby toward the lifts as we sat for afternoon refreshments.

"This guy better be good," said a charming voice from behind our perch. "Uncle Sam!" Anna Marie gushed. "You could have come back sooner," she whispered, politely hugging me and pecking my cheeks. "Meet my husband, Anders," she stepped back to offer my acquaintance.

If Andreas had looked anything like this manifestation of an ancient god, I would be jealous. Tall, lithe, elegant, golden, and charming. I would have felt inferior. Hansi was, thankfully, greeting Anna Marie with their sibling ritual of joking, poking fun, hugs, and kisses.

Before we ordered cakes and beverages for them, Anders got to the point. "We have submitted preliminary paperwork to the state for the Trust. That should be enough to ward off any attempts to interfere."

Hansi translated Austrian legalese that I didn't understand. We noted a few suggestions for tweaks and thanked Anders for his quick and thorough work.

Business out of the way, I responded to Anna Marie's initial greeting. "Fred has a voice you will not believe."

"I've heard a lot of voices over the years, Uncle Sam. Let me be the judge of that."

"Mutti and Vatti Steiner—."

"Ah, you are already on familial title status," she said. She looked to Hansi and Anders.

"Don't get all protective," Hansi said. "They like Sam because he apologized for his initial rude behavior." He stroked my shin under the table.

"I didn't know who they were at the time of my insolence." I tried to get her to laugh. Anders seemed fine with it all.

"My mother?" She asked in defiance.

"Frau Wortmann. But she insisted I call her Adelheid. What was I to do?"

"Come back when you said you would."

"Anna Marie, don't," said Hansi. "Sam and I are good."

"Now. Do you know the pain you caused my brother. And my mother? You were family and you walked away."

"He's here now, meine Schwester. Another time, perhaps."

"Anna Marie," I said. "I am sorry I hurt you. Frau Wortmann and I have met and healed our wound. I hope we can, too."

Anders stepped in, "Perhaps we can come to Salzburg soon. You can talk then if you are both inclined."

If Andreas was as politic and diplomatic as Anders, I would be jealous.

"How, when he is leaving in a few days," she said.

I kicked Hansi under the table.

"He's coming back," Hansi interjected. "Can we change the subject."

"Hans—. Uncle Sam, look me in the eyes and tell me you won't hurt my brother like you did before."

"Anna Marie," Hansi said. "Sam told me he is coming back. I believe him. It would be helpful if you would, too."

"When it happens, I'll believe him." Her looks were killing me. "Now, tell me about this voice you have all of Vienna nattering about." She pulled several fliers out of her satchel. It was only then I noticed her violin case. She saw me smile then reached across the table to squeeze my hand. "I missed you, too, Uncle Sam."

"Mutti's handiwork," said Hansi, scrutinizing the flyers front and back. "I wonder how many strings she pulled to get this done so fast."

Anders added, "And distributed around the city so thoroughly. We spotted them a few days ago in cafés and coffee shops out by us."

We unpacked what Mutti Steiner was up to. While it was slowly being revealed, we discussed what may or may not be sprung this evening, particularly discussing Gunther and his potential disruptive options.

Anna Marie went upstairs to ready Mutti Wortmann.

Anders followed shortly after to check on the Steiners.

Hansi and I retreated to our room to refresh.

We were fiddling with each other's clothes heading toward a quickie and a shared shower when Hansi's mobile interrupted. We ignored the first call. The second one, he glanced at the bedside table to see who was calling.

"Fred, how is the rehearsal going?" He put him on speaker.

"He's threatened Margarette if she sings tonight. He said he'll destroy her. She's in tears. She's afraid. We can't do this tonight."

"Is Gunter there?" Hansi said.

"He left. It was awful."

"Are you and Margarette in a safe place?"

"We're on the stage."

"We'll be there in twenty minutes. Is there security?"

"Yes."

"Tell them only Sam and I enter until this is resolved. Can you do that, Fred?"

"Yes."

"Twenty minutes. It will work out, Fred. Twenty minutes."

I had the shower going and fresh clothes laid out. We were out the door in seven. Hansi called Anders on the way. He would gather Mutti Wortmann and alert his parents.

The one scenario we did not anticipate was the one Gunther parried.

"Game on," I said, as we dived into a cab.

Security did their job until Fred collected us.

We had two hours to put Margarette back together, to help Fred focus, and find another accompanist because the pianist was too shaken to do the evening justice.

We wondered what Gunther would have for us next.

We got them up to rehearse, which shifted their emotions. If they could sustain that, their Lieder would be gorgeous.

Thirty minutes later, Mutti and Vatti Steiner pushed through the doors with security following in their wake, followed by food delivery people after that. Vatti brushed away security with his raised hand, his walking stick flailing.

"What happened?" Mutti Steiner said, halfway up the aisle.

Herr Steiner tried to slow her down.

"What has he done?" she continued.

The accompanist excused himself and bolted.

Margarette sat, her dejection palpable.

Frau Steiner went to her and urged her to the wings.

"We need a backup plan," I said to Hansi and Herr Steiner.

"Katarin and I have that ready."

"What is it," Hansi said before I could.

"Let us wait to see if we need it."

172

He went to Fred who stood stiff and dejected and pulled him to the piano. He sat and began the first Lied on the program, which was a male solo. Fred's stiffness graduated to erect confidence. His shaking voice elevated to strong tones.

"He'll be fine," Hansi whispered. "It's Margarette—."

The second Lied on the program was the female solo. We turned to the wings.

Frau Steiner re-entered holding Margarette's hand. She encouraged the young soprano with a nod of her head, and joined Herr Steiner on key and time, holding the youth's shaking hand throughout. Katarin glanced our way, her fear unmissable.

Fred and Margarette took a break and the four of us conferred.

"She won't make it through. She's too shaken," Mutti Steiner said.

"Vatti, what is your plan," asked Hansi.

Anton looked at Katarin who was talking to the young singers. We could not hear.

"Vatti?"

"Patience. Trust. Anticipation."

The foodies hadn't unloaded their carry bags. They were probably music students themselves and enthralled by the presence of Salzburg legends. I shifted to help them and discreetly invited them back for the recital, not least to ensure proper service.

After a very quiet meal, Fred and Margarette went backstage to dress and prepare.

"One thing is certain," said Vatti Steiner. "I am the accompanist tonight."

Katarin leaned against him, taking his hands, massaging them for a few minutes.

I had to ask, "Can Margarette perform?"

"She said yes. We shall see." Mutti Steiner looked conspiratorial and uncertain. "We will know when she sings her first bar." Her eyebrows rose and fell, perhaps remembering her own early struggles with stage fears; the difference, no doubt, that Gunther had unleased a tirade of insult to undermine young courage.

Not long after, Frau Wortmann arrived with Anna Marie on her arm and Anders behind. We offered food but they had eaten at the hotel. They took their seats in the second row. Anna Marie fussed. Adelheid let her. Anders offered us his assistance.

Guests arrived. Mutti and Vatti Steiner greeted many of them; several earnest-looking ones formed a brief knot around them then melted toward their reserved seats. Mutti's knot of secrecy was unraveling a little at a time.

No sign of the evening's nemesis.

The audience tittered when Herr Anton Steiner mounted the stage followed by his soloist of many years, both beaming as if they hadn't abandoned performing a decade before.

We helped the delivery kids through security and up to the front row, glancing at the newly unknotted, whispering animatedly. Hansi and I shifted our seating arrangements to the last row, to prevent disruption to the recital if needed.

The first half started promptly at 7:00 p.m. and bumped along, Fred and Margarette relaxing and settling into their music. Herr Steiner accompanied robustly and appropriately, Frau Steiner the celebrity page turner. The performance garnered a tepid response.

The twenty-minute break started at 7:50 p.m. The performers retreated to the wings to relax, and probably for a pep talk from Mutti Steiner.

We joined attendees in the lobby where we discovered an audience of a different sort in progress, complete with shouting and arm tossing.

Gunther held court. Or was it an uprising?

He caught sight of us and pushed his gaggle and others aside.

"What is the meaning of this?" His eyes were wide.

Hansi stepped where I was ready to pounce, "Is something amiss, Herr Drecker?"

"Don't patronize me." He brandished an oversized invitation for all to see. "I was assured this event began at 8:00 p.m., yet I arrive to find that I am sequestered from the music I love and the musicians I nurtured. That is what is amiss, Herr Wortmann."

I wanted to shout Halleluiah! for Mutti Steiner's subterfuge but I restrained my glee. Hansi's hands rapidly opened and closed, suppressing the same joy as best he could.

"It would appear you have incorrect information," Hansi said.

"Indeed, and one wonders who is behind this skullduggery, this insult, this provocation." He snorted his growing anger and frisbeed the envelope to the wall.

While we ogled Gunter and his gang, others joined the widening circle. His eyes narrowed in recognition of some of the joiners. One of them stepped forward.

"Herr Drecker," the smartly dressed woman started, "how does it feel to have one of your protégés stolen from you so publicly?"

"Ah, my dear, so lovely to see you again. Thank you for the lovely article you placed in the Linzer Oberösterreichische Nachrichten. Always an honor."

"Your response, please." The reporter held firm.

"No one steals protégés, my dear. Herr Gluck can arrange his own recitals."

"It is my understanding that Herr und Frau Steiner are his teachers and they made these arrangements for him. Does that not constitute a loss to you?"

Recorders and phones thrust through the growing crowd. Younger attendees filmed the exchange.

Another voice shouted from behind the wall of the curious. "We understand you berated Fräulein Margarette Horner before the recital. Is that how you support your protégés, Herr Drecker? By calling the females whores and the males, traitors?"

"Who is that? I know that voice. Show yourself. I demand it."

Fred took two strides into the circle.

The assembly gasped and tittered.

Gunther stepped back.

Arms encircled my waist and a chin rested on my shoulder. I tried to turn but was held fast.

"This dustup has the smell of an American attorney at law. Brilliant move, maestro. I'd applaud but I think my intentions are clear." Rheinhardt squeezed his approval.

"Not my doing, Rheinhardt. Your father is going to expel you from the family business if you don't stop taking breaks."

"Closed for a week," he said.

"In the height of tourist season?"

"Water damage from a flood upstairs. Job secure, Herr Greyling."

"Our friendship is secure as well. However, you are overstepping at the moment."

His squeeze softened.

"Much like our rotund friend?" He sniggered as quietly as he could, not wanting to upset Herr Drecker who was sputtering in self-defense.

Another reporter stepped into the fray.

"Are all the Nachtrichtens here?" Gunther squeaked a smile.

"Will you confirm with us, Herr Drecker, that you ply your protégés with certain substances at lavish parties at your home in Salzburg. Will you confirm that favors are required for your assistance? Will you further confirm that your protégés' parents are required to support you in certain ways?"

Gunther turned on his heals.

"How insulting. How demeaning can you be with such talented youth and their families seeking success for their children. How despicable this affair is."

He stopped and turned to me. Rheinhart released me and slunk away. Hansi stepped beside me.

"Him. They." He pointed in our direction, bejeweled fingers pulsating.

We waited for accusations.

"They are out to ruin me!"

Herr und Frau Steiner entered the circle, standing beside Fred.

The crowd silenced. Mutti Steiner stepped forward and turned in an elegant circle looking at each person. She stopped at Gunther.

"Young musicians," she started, in her small voice projected as if on a grand stage, "wish to learn from those who understand what it takes to be successful in this industry. Austria, and indeed Salzburg, is a magnet for world class performers. One person, or one method of training, cannot assist all students of music, who are free to explore the wide panoply of teachers and methods. Anton and I encourage exploration. We support expansion of music learning and performance opportunities. This evening, we have offered two students the opportunity to perform for a knowledgeable and inquisitive audience. We are happy to assist them as best we can."

Gunther huffed. Fred relaxed. Vatti Steiner stepped next to his wife.

"We thank all of you for coming this evening," he swept his arm around the circle ending at Gunther. "The second half of the performance holds surprises and wonders. I invite you all to take your seats while the performers prepare. We apologize that the evening will be extended somewhat."

He and Mutti Steiner walked regally back into the hall as if they were the centers of attention at the Vienna Opera Ball.

Fred stopped in front of us. "This evening will go down in history."

Hansi and I stood guard as the crowd returned to their seats.

Gunther shooed his gaggle out the doors. His defiant stance already said what he nonetheless spoke. "This is not over. I abhor humiliation. I abhor those who humiliate. This will continue, my friends. You will rue the day."

He stared at us, sniffed, and stomped out. We could see him dismiss his toys with a flick of his wrist then disappear into the night. Rheinhart followed, slumped and dejected.

I grabbed Hansi's hand. "Enjoy tonight. Deal with him tomorrow."

"I'm not sure any amount of diplomacy will stop him anytime soon."

"Tomorrow, mein Herz. Let's see what surprises and wonders your in-laws have prepared."

Hansi did a quick check on Mutti Wortmann and then we plunked into our seats.

Herr Steiner strode from the wings.

"Meine Damen und Herren, there is a change in the program for the second part of the performance. Fräulein Horner will assist me at piano. Herr Gluck will be accompanied by Frau Katarin Steiner. Please enjoy your evenings."

Margarette joined Herr Steiner at the piano and they quickly reviewed his preferences for page turning. They waited, as did the audience, which had begun chattering before Vatti Steiner had finished his first sentence.

I joined in the titter-tatter to Hansi, "This will be excellent." I grabbed his hand and held on tight.

As an overture, Herr Steiner started with the music from the last Lied from the first half. As he completed that, Fred escorted Mutti Steiner to the stage. With a flourish, they both bowed, to the delight and ample applause of the audience. Media photographers danced around the room taking photos from all angles. Lights flashed. Frau Steiner glowed. Fred looked a tad overwhelmed and daunted.

He missed his first note. Herr Steiner stopped. Frau Steiner took his hands as she had when they'd sung three weeks before. Her steady gaze calmed her new protégé and she motioned for Anton to begin again.

Fred didn't miss a note, a pause, an interval of harmony, a glissando, or a smile of gratitude to his soprano. The audience passed through appreciation to adoration. At the end, their applause might have been heard in Salzburg.

Frau Steiner stepped back allowing Fred to bask in his triumph. He knew much of the applause was for the Steiners, but he didn't let that stop him from a long series of bows. He had the presence of mind to acknowledge Herr and Frau Steiner, and to bring Margarette to the front to share in the moment. In a few short weeks, Mutti Steiner had transformed Fred into a performer with grace, humility, and professional stage presence.

Mutti Steiner was not prepared for the pace at which reviews appeared on the internet.

"We should at least be able to celebrate the evening before the reviews hammer us," she sighed and laughed with delight.

We had avoided the Sacre Hotel, knowing our little recital would be overwhelmed by opera, symphony, ballet, and other performance audiences.

Margarette took the nine of us to a small lounge across the Ring from the venue. Hansi went in first to make certain Gunther and his gaggle weren't lurking. We found comfortable seating for the elders. Fred and Margarette were given places of honor. The rest of us stood about.

Fred's social media started pinging first, then Margarette's. These were posts of the exchanges with Gunther from different angles and with varying comments from the youth perspective. Memes flew around their followers and friends, funny and tragic with each chortle they inspired.

Hansi said, "Rheinhart will make sure Gunther sees this storm of humiliation."

"We might need to join social media to see the horror," I chuckled.

The news sites followed soon after.

'Frederic Gluck Triumphs in the Light of Katarin Steiner's Return' and *'The Steiners Introduce the Next Gen of Classical Talent'* and *'Frederic Gluck Storms into the Light the Steiners Create.'*

Vatti Steiner patted Fred on the hand. "Don't let it go to your head, mein Sohn. They will turn on you the first chance they get."

"Vatti, let the young man enjoy his first of many triumphs," said Hansi, sliding his arm around Fred's neck for support.

Margarette had received minor mentions in the articles read so far. Mutti Steiner said to her softly, "My dear, the world is waiting for you, too. We will make sure they hear only you very soon."

Vatti Steiner agreed wholeheartedly. "We will discuss your training before we return to Salzburg, if you wish."

Hansi whispered to me, "What have we done?"

"They seem ten years younger," I returned.

"It may fall to you and me to rein them in. Pace their work. They are excited in the moment. Tomorrow morning, we will know what they are able to do."

I squeezed his hand in agreement and reassurance.

What I didn't do was remind him we needed a new strategy for dealing with Gunther Drecker, whose promise of reprisal I took seriously.

It was a tortured train ride home to Castle Getreidegasse and a restless night.

None of us were prepared for what came next.

Fifteen

Back in Salzburg, after delivering Mutti Wortmann back to her castle in the forest, we gathered at the Steiners' home.

Mutti and Vatti Steiner dragged themselves into the house. Hansi insisted they nap for twenty minutes. Fred started on a late lunch but once I saw that his cooking was a student's answer to food, I pulled him back out to the local shops to build a grazing buffet fit for the royals he was now tethered to for the rest of his career.

He still buzzed from his performance and aftermath, checking his phone and saying 'wow' every ten minutes.

We were about to wake the Steiners for lunch when there was a strenuous banging on the street level door.

Hansi glanced out the window but reported nothing. "I'll go down," he said, twitching his head indicating I should join him.

"Perhaps you left this at the hotel, Herr Greyling." Georg Stohl thrust a large envelope in my direction. Hansi reached for it. "I am to deliver this into Herr Greyling's hands." He lifted his snout in defiance.

"If you are to deliver it, Georg, then I can surmise I didn't leave it at the hotel, nicht war?" I said, not taking the envelope still hanging off his extended arm.

"Perhaps it is important," he said.

"To someone, I am sure it is," I said.

"You aren't at work," Hansi said.

Defiantly holding his arm in place, Georg retorted, "Doing the work of others is my work."

Deadlocked. I leaned against the door jamb.

"Just take the damn thing, will you," Georg shouted.

He let go when Hansi grasped it.

"Thank you," Hansi said. "We'll be sure to drop a gratuity by the hotel."

Georg climbed into Gunther's car. "Not to bother. There will be a car for you at 7:00 p.m. this evening. Bring Herr Gluck, please."

With the car out of sight, Hansi tore the envelope open.

He laughed so loud he apologized to a couple walking their yapping dog.

"An audience, it would seem. Offering a truce." He flipped through several pages. "He acts fast. It's a legal document."

"What?"

"Seems he is trying 'nice' before he unleashes his attorneys."

"Shit."

The previous night was catching up to me. I needed a nap.

"Don't say anything to Fred or Mutti and Vatti. This is our battle."

"Fred is going to need an outlet for his energy. Youth and success gotta be expressed. What can we do?" I said, closing the door behind us.

"We'll figure it out." Hansi pecked my cheek. "Give Mutti and Vatti a chance to create something."

"He could be drawn back into that scene Drecker has created."

"Let's ask." Hani's wisdom won the mood game.

"Wait." I countered wisdom with fact. "You didn't want to tell them."

"A nap before engagement will sort out the fact that I am allowed to change." He tweaked my chin as if I were a pre-teen asking about sex and being told that all would become clear soon. I batted him away with a playful snort.

We told Fred and the in-laws what had occurred. They chuckled about the absurdity of the delivery and the outlandishness of what had been proposed.

Vatti summed it up. "We continue Fred's instruction in addition to his classes. We create opportunities to build his exposure. You two deal with Herr Drecker and work on the Trust. Anything more complicated will disrupt Fred's focus."

I added, "We must acknowledge that Fred needs additional outlets for creativity that keep him from the temptations Gunther offers."

"Thanks, Dad," Fred chimed. "I will take care of myself." He looked to Hansi for support.

"He'll come at you from all sides." Hansi's support was as skinny as Fred's jeans.

"I'm not going to hide or run away. This town is too small."

"You are not going this evening, if that's what you are angling for," Hansi interjected.

"I faced him down yesterday." He had a point.

I started to think the best defense was an offense more robust than the antagonists.

"Look," I proposed. "I need a nap. Let's think on it for an hour. Meet back here for more grazing and thinking aloud. I'm inclined to agree with Fred."

Hansi looked resigned to the mathematics of the argument.

I concluded, "We gotta think more broadly about what Gunther might do. I hadn't guessed he'd go after Margarette."

Polite to almost rude became part of our strategy. Fred, Hansi and I knocked on the mansion door at 7:19 p.m. under the gaze of the suffering Sebastian.

"Beautiful," I remarked at the intoxicating view back toward Salzburg and the Untersberg.

"Focus, would you please," Hansi said. "That mountain isn't going anywhere."

The door swept open to reveal Gunther in a suit, conservative in color, coordinated from shoes to tie, serious in intent. His hair was composed to an inch of its perfection, salt and pepper rather than his usual unnatural show.

His hand, with single ring, dangled in front of him with his pinky finger reacting.

"My friends." Controlled and controlling. "Please come in. We are gathered poolside. A quiet evening, I hope."

We walked through the foyer and he said in a respectful tone to no one we could see, "Our drinks, please."

The pool lights were soft white, plants underlit similarly. A Mozart string quartet played on a hidden sound system. Light and temperate in mood.

"Please, join us here," Gunther indicated with a flow of his hand, not the usual twist of wrist.

"Before we begin," he said, "I would like to congratulate Herr Gluck for his bravura performance in Vienna last evening. While I was prevented from hearing it in my person, the reviews have been stellar. Your brief work with Herr und Frau Steiner has been rewarded. What do you have to say, Frederic?"

Drinks arrived and the timing annoyed Gunther. He bore down on his attempt to not show his pique. The new, brunette toy boy was not yet up to snuff. I wondered where blondie had been sent for reprogramming.

Hansi and I took sips of our three-finger single malts. The highest quality, 75 years of contemplation on what scotch could be.

Fred leaned forward to push his crystal liter of Stiegl away. An inch of contempt. Point made.

"What would you prefer, Frederic? A very dry martini? An American whiskey? A Shirley Temple?" Gunther's façade was melting.

"Perhaps you can tell us why you wish to speak to us," I said.

His entire pile of flesh turned to me. A moment. A touch to his forehead without his usual handkerchief. He seemed perplexed that it wasn't there. A moment more.

"I understand," he started, "that you received an envelope this afternoon. Surely you humored me by studying it?"

Hansi stepped in. "Sorry, we forgot it. We glanced through it. I know I am a little confused." He looked at me. I blinked agreement over my turned-up grin.

Fumes built behind Gunther's eyes.

Hansi turned to Fred, "What would you like to drink, my friend?"

"A single malt would be lovely, thank you," Fred replied.

Gunther shot a look at the brunette who scurried to the inside bar. He wasn't as slender and tight as the blond. Downsizing. Media scrutiny.

"Summarize for us," I asked Gunther.

He composed himself like a zen master.

Fred's drink arrived. The brunette rested his hand on Fred's shoulder while placing the four fingered glass on a coaster on the table.

Gunther's delight was imperceptible, except to the three of us.

Fred took the attendant's hand. "Would you be so kind as to bring us some ice water. Perhaps a nibble or two?"

The startled rabbit shot a look at Gunther.

"I had hoped you would dine with me at eight." Gunther surveyed our faces. "Yes. Go. Go. Go. French canapes." He waived his hand in his familiar fashion. "We have a dinner engagement," Hansi lied. "Eight thirty in town. We snacked before we hailed the cab." Hansi taunted further. "I read the word transparency in your missive."

"Stop it or I'll throw you all out. Then sue the crap out of you." Gunther stood. "You stole my protégé and have been lurking around others for weeks. They signed contracts. Their parents signed contracts. They are liable for my services. I will collect any way I can." He pointed my direction. "It's all your fault, Sam. You did this. You came back. You fucked this up."

He was right. If I hadn't returned, no one would have known what he was doing. I wouldn't have met Fred. Hansi would have been stuck in his grief too deeply to see it even if he had hooked up with Fred or another of Gunther's grifts. It was all my fault.

"Sit down, Gunther. You are right. I am the bad guy," I said. "Except you are feeding off music students, their families, and the charitable and social structures of Salzburg. You have become bored with empire and so you play with people's lives without agreeing boundaries. Your boundaries are the grift that is known to you alone. That is the thing with unscrupulous people, they do it in the dark behind happy rhetoric, not so innocent parties, and distant sources of cash. What you have built is unsustainable because parents start to ask questions, gossip becomes fact, and honor has no value. You abandoned your search for respect by buying favor, pretty people, and perpetrating lies."

I rested my case. Hansi stroked my shin with his foot.

Fred leaned forward to look at me, "You are so hot when you talk attorney."

"Shut up, Frederic," Gunther said.

French canapes arrived but the host flicked the brunette away before he could serve them, let alone flirt with any of us.

"I can see that my offer to repair this situation will go nowhere." He stood.

I downed my scotch. Hansi took a gulp of his.

Fred said, "Do you have a forever cup I could take this in." He lifted his glass as he stood.

"You will hear from my attorneys. They will begin proceedings against your family, Herr Gluck. Put that down and leave this instant." He directed Fred with the wand that his arm had become.

"Thank you for your continued hospitality," Fred bowed, deep and long.

Gunther grabbed Fred's drink and flung the contents over him.

Fred stood tall, "I wish to thank you for your assistance, Herr Drecker. You were a gentleman of note until I was enlightened by Herr und Frau Steiner. I will always remember what you did to me."

Hansi grabbed Fred's arm. "Let's get some fresh air."

No brunette toy boy opened the door for us.

Our cab waited as we had hoped. None of us fancied a five mile walk to town or a wait for another cab. Saint Sebastian was not a happy companion.

"Still worried about me?" Fred said sitting back in the cab.

"Damn the consequences is one approach," I said.

Hansi laughed. "You were brilliant. I hope Anders knows a few attorneys."

We drove the rest of the way in silence, contentment illuding me as I dropped into more memories of choices made long ago.

Sixteen

Memories started with my own pique of near contempt. "Why aren't you upset," I shouted.

We were in Leon's love nest that was now a tentative, I'm-not-sure-what-to-do nest of vipers and dangers and me turning into a tourist who had a fling in a town with a medieval castle and music everywhere. "At least beg me to stay. Tell me I'm wrong. Call my parents and tell *them* to go to hell. Something, Hansi!"

His naked torso rippled as he pulled himself up to the headboard rearranging pillows so he could lounge with his arms above his head, his pits exposed, his pubic hairs teasing above the duvet cover.

"I should have told you after sex," I said, turning away fighting the urge to change my mind. "You said yourself that getting the visa was going to be more complicated. The consulate was clear that I'd have to leave the country for weeks to apply for permanent status. You were with me. You heard her say the better option was to go back to the States because these things take time."

He rearranged his legs so more pubic hair glared at me. I wanted him to glare at me. I wanted him angry as fuck so this would be easier.

"I can abandon the pre-paid tour of southern Europe to get us two more weeks. I'll be back for a couple of days if I don't. I'll be here for a few nights before my train to Ostend. I need to thank Leon for his hospitality even though I'm paying him with my last Schillings." I chuckled. He didn't.

His left leg escaped the pressures of the duvet. He crooked it so his dick and balls flopped toward me.

I sat on the edge of the bed as far from him as I could get but within touching distance. Within the distance it would take me to lay down and blow him. Within distance of throwing caution to the wind and declaring that I was going to stay come high water or hell freezing my balls off.

His leg slowly lay flat against the bed. He had helped me lose my inhibitions. He had taught me ways of being sexual I would not have discovered in ten years of trying back in the States.

"Back in the States," I said. Trying it on for size and watching the size of his dick expand.

"Back in the States, I can finish my degree and work on my German. I can come back as soon as that is done. Two years. Three max. We can wait for each other. That will be about the time you finish your medical degree."

His other leg scrunched the duvet against me. I placed my hand to stop the tide of it as he pushed it harder.

"You could come to America to get an advanced degree. There must be universities that would grant you the money. Johns Hopkins. Stanford. Northwestern. They all take foreign students."

I was running out of negotiating. I was definitely out of self-control. I leaned over to fondle him. His dick and balls soft but not soft. His furry legs. His gut with more hair than my entire body.

He reached out and forced me down on him.

"Stop talking, Greyling. We have one night to fuck so get to it."

Between gasps for air, I said, "You aren't mad?"

While he arched his back and writhed in delight he said, "Angry as fuck, which is why you are going to get the fuck of your life so if you never come back, you'll know how much I care."

Wait. What?

"I'm coming back," I sat up to deliver that line of import. "It's not if, it's when. Hansi, I'm coming back."

He pushed me off his leg and stood up, dick stiff but losing the battle with gravity.

"Can you guarantee you'll be back?" He asked, legs wide, arms pinched into his sides.

"Do you have a plan in place to make it happen? Do you know what it will take? You can complete your degree here. Your German is excellent. You told me you were going to change your degree anyway. Change it here. Vatti will give you a job. You can live alone, maybe with Leon, or move in with them. Anna Marie would love to have you around."

He paced. I sat. I waited.

"Instead of me moving to America you could move to Innsbruck. It's too late now to go explore their degree offers because you are off to study Greece and Italy for weeks. If you were serious about our plans, you would have demanded we do that. Did you even explore what the University of Salzburg offers? Did you speak with admissions like I suggested? No, you did not. Stupid fuck, me, for not seeing a month ago that your plans were different from mine. Stupid fuck me for believing you told your parents, and they were 'OK' with it." Air quotes meant he was really hacked off.

"I thought you wanted to fuck me so I'd remember you into the next century," I said.

"That's how long it will take you to return, Greyling. An old, fat American tourist unable to remember this city or anything we did together. Your promise to return is hollow. I will only believe it when it happens."

"We'll write. An occasional phone call won't cost so much. We'll figure it out."

"We already figured it out!"

"Technically we didn't. I said I'd stay—."

"And now you aren't.

191

"Hansi, we both knew the whole thing was tentative at best. My musical translated to a few months of fun. Your film noir of hope. Would it even work without the adrenaline of possible and the passion of desire. Look me in the eye and tell me you were confident we would succeed if I stayed."

"That's the whole point, you stupid fuck," he said running his hand down his face, then back up into his hair. His lovely thick hair. "I'm sorry. You aren't stupid. But you are fucked. Damn you fucking bastard. The whole point is the trying. The point is to work at it so it does succeed. Why did I fall in love with a stupid American? I'm sorry, in this you are stupid. We figured it out and now you are telling me you changed your mind."

I turned to the window. Natural light was fading, which meant the klieg light of revelations would shout into our growing darkness.

"I didn't change my mind. It got changed by circumstances."

"Don't patronize me, Greyling. You knew the first day we met at the pub that I didn't cop to that shit."

He moved behind me, placed one hand on my shoulder, the other on the side of my head, moving it around to my face. He inserted fingers into my mouth. His other hand circled down my chest to find my nipple. I leaned against his tease and foreplay. I reached behind to cup him in both hands. I felt him swelling into my crack. He rocked forward and back. My head rested between his neck and his shoulder. The heat grew. The friction. The frisson. This simple easy manner made him come between my legs. He flipped me around and went down on me. The silken wetness stroked my hardness. His gentle squeezing pulsed my nuts. He used hand and mouth to lengthen the pleasure. I exploded down his throat. He stood and kissed me. The taste of us lolled in my mouth. I licked his tongue and lips.

We kissed our way to the bed, shoving the duvet to the floor.

It wasn't long before he was ready for more. My own hesitated but joined the party when needed.

He was true to his promise. He fucked me to the edge of my life. He fucked me twice more to imprint on my memory. When he couldn't fuck, we slept. Time slipped away.

We didn't say goodbye when morning rudely separated us. He stayed at Leon's, forcing me into a walk of shame past his house. I ran to my student room to shower, pack, and join the group for our last lunch together in the Center.

My nostalgic walk through the back garden didn't help. Hansi and his family sat on their patio over their own lunch. It was evident he'd told them. I waved but each in their own way ignored me. Entering through the back door of the Center for the last time, I turned to see Hansi standing where I had first seen him, when I pretended to look at the Untersberg in the distance. I paused. He did not turn away as he might have.

Our train left at 3:00 p.m. so we'd see the mountains of southern Austria before the darkness of Yugoslavia. After our tour of southern Europe, I did, indeed, stay three nights at Leon's waiting for my departure to Ostende, London, and home. During the days, I revisited our haunts. At night I remembered every moment of being fucked to the edge of life, where I thought I might wait forever.

At the station I kept looking behind hoping Hansi would come to say goodbye.

As the train left Salzburg, I started my new life. Waiting. On the edge.

Seventeen

The next morning in real time, the intensity of Vienna along with the immersion into families Wortmann and Steiner weighed on me. The necessity of the Trust to help young musicians created tension, where prior to my return I had none to speak of except the mental and emotional recovery from the grief and loss of Thomas.

The end of my second visit to Salzburg was fast approaching. I had to consider what was waiting for me back home.

Back home.

What was that for me?

My arguments of the past didn't hold water because I was no longer beholden to parents, family, or a partner. I was no longer a student clamoring to decide on a future path bolstered by one or more academic degrees. I was no longer duct-taped to a career that had been fulfilling when working, but lacking when thoughts of my choices filled my down time.

I grappled with the question of Thomas and how much he would and should influence my choices now. I wanted to let go but I wanted him close. He meant too much to let him float away.

These thoughts happened on my way from Getreidegasse to the Steiners. I stood on the bridge looking down at the water flowing beneath. The same log was stuck behind the pylon. The mighty Salzach raged around the calm catchpoint. I wanted to throw a huge rock at the log to dislodge it, to free it, to move it along. I also wondered how long it had survived stuck in one place, held fast because the forces around it didn't allow it to float free.

"I understand you will be joining us for dinner in a few days, Herr Greyling." Rheinhart sidled next to me. "What are you looking at down there?" He peered over the bridge. "Ha. I wonder how many people have seen a metaphor for themselves in that old thing. It's smaller than it used to be when I was younger."

"How long has it been there."

"My parents tease that they almost named me Holzstamm." My quizzical face made him laugh louder. "I thought you were fluent, Sam. It means wooden log in my humble language. Of course," he hazarded another glance downward, "they could have called me Durchnasst, which would have been worse, I suppose."

He saw I was still puzzled.

"Transliterated to woder logd. Now do you get it?"

"Well, Holtzstamm woder logd, what brings you this direction? On a mission for Gunther?"

"That's not nice, Sam," he smiled.

"You appeared in Vienna with some cock-assed story about a flood in your restaurant. On my walk this morning I saw no evidence of repairs being made."

He hemmed, searching for a haw, then stuttered to a stop.

"Since I met you, I have been curious about what you want to do with your life," I said.

"Seems to be a stuck log for several of us." He leaned back against the bridge railing and crossed his arms.

"Are the culinary arts in your future? Managing a restaurant of high quality? Fucking Gunther and his toys?"

"That last one was low, Sam," he smiled. "I understand why you'd ask that question because you had your fling in Salzburg then threw it away. The difference between you and me, Herr Greyling, is that I enjoy life as it comes. You grieve about what might have been. Like our log down there, you are stuck. I'm going to bet you don't have the guts to change."

He patted me on the back and strode over the rest of the bridge. I watched him head toward Mirabell assuming a meeting with Gunther or a sex thing with one of the captive students. What do I know.

Rather than ponder the log of my life, I looked up at Hohensalzburg then over to Kapuzinerberg then followed the flow of the Salzach back into the salted hills alive with music. I followed that line into my past life here and wondered what that past gave me in my current state of stuck.

After five ponderous minutes, I scuffled off to the Steiners to check on Fred, my agreed task for the day. Hansi was on calls with Anders and a friendly attorney about the Trust. We'd agreed dinner at the Greek place around 6:00 p.m. I had a few hours to flay.

I heard the hubbub as I turned the corner.

A TV truck, a radio transmitter looking ancient and out of place, and ten or twelve people milled about outside the Steiners home. Where it had been calm on day one after Vienna, day two was a melee of media. I crossed the street and sauntered up to the first person craning their neck toward the door. I was taller and wanted to tell him there was nothing to see here so go the fuck home.

"What's going on," I said as near to a Salzburg dialect as I could muster.

"Trying to get that wunderkind and the Steiner woman for interviews," he said without looking at me, which wouldn't have helped him anyway because I was unknown to them. I planned to keep it that way.

I walked a few meters down the short alley nearby. Fred picked up on the first ring or buzz or sonata he had assigned as my ring tone.

"Sam, this is nuts. Where are you? Can you get in? We can't get out. They've been here for hours."

"Slow down, Fred. Have any of you said anything to them?"

"No! They showed up and started banging on the door around 7:00."

"Do you need anything? Coffee? Food?"

"I couldn't get my double cappuccino macchiato with cinnamon and extra cream. Anton wants his daily newspaper, that local one, you know what he likes, right? We need fruit. And milk. Katarin is asking for a selection of pastries—."

"Tell them I'll do their weekly grocery shop, too. I'll get what I can. Watch for me out the window so I don't have to knock."

I bumbled through the shops and an American coffee chain as quickly as I could.

Getting through the scrum without spilling, dropping, or scrunching anything was a challenge. Fred saw me coming and I was in before any of the gossip hordes got a look at me.

Mutti Steiner's hug was delicate compared to Mutti Wortmann's vice grip. I welcomed it with reassurances.

They scarfed coffees, pastries and fruit as if food would disappear from the earth by 4:00 p.m.

"They are in my socials," said Fred.

"Go dark for 48 hours. Everything. Off. Out. Done. Whatever word you use for not using your socials," I said.

"My friends?"

"Tell 'em why afterwards. Don't tell 'em now because the media are in there."

"Mutti." The first time I used the familiar to her face. "Can your PR people help? I'm not adept at media control."

"Excellent." She was on it.

I tried Hansi but he was engaged on one of his scheduled calls. I texted him with a semi-urgent request to get his ass over here and he could do his calls from here.

I ventured a glance between the sheer curtains. The crowd had not dispersed but a cop car was now parked in the alley. Standing back from the flashing blue lights, tucked in a doorway and visible when he poked his head out, was our friend Rheinhart. I watched him for a few seconds. Each glance our way was accompanied by a smile of his newly whitened teeth, bared more like an alley cat's than a breed from Cheshire.

This was a skirmish in Gunther's war. We now had an objective to overcome.

"Game on," I whispered to myself.

"What do you mean?" Mutti Steiner said from behind.

I startled. "Herr Drecker brought this upon us, Mutti. One of his spies is out there."

"Who is that?"

"No one of note."

"Everyone is of note, Sam Greyling." Her resolution was charming and devious. That combination served her well in interpreting music. It was obviously getting her through life, as well. I wondered if we needed her PR people or if we could unleash her on the throngs.

An idea formed. I needed Hansi and Mutti S. to work it through. It might work. It might blow the whole thing out of the water.

"Tell me the name of the spy," she persisted.

When I told her, she smiled her devious charm.

She poked Vatti Steiner's daily paper to startle him into battle. "We've got 'game on'," she sang, his scorn appearing over the top of the paper. "Herr Drecker is at it again, Anton, mein Herz."

Christ, I thought. Hansi and I are sounding like them.

Schatz und Herz and everything sweet and loving. A long way from all those years before when our endearments edged on taunts and insults, as one does in youth. I meandered through my memories.

Shouting from the streets pulled me back to problems at hand.

"Herr Wortmann."

"Herr Wortmann, may I have a word?"

Herr Wortmann this and Herr Wortmann that and Herr Wortmann when and Herr Wortmann now.

He slid through the crack of the opened door.

"What the fuck?"

"Wonderful to see you, too," I chortled through my peck on his tender, wet lips.

"Seriously, what the fuck is this?"

"Gunther."

"Game on!" he proclaimed.

Mutti Steiner tweaked the paper again. Vatti S. didn't bother displaying pique. He flipped the paper back in place and continued his morning routine.

"Hans, it's 'game on' with that Drecker fellow. Isn't it exciting?"

"No, it's not exciting." Fred chomped on his last bite of pastry and slurped his coffee. "He's cornered and he fears his empire will crumble. We need to be careful."

"We need to do what's right." Mutti S. wrapped her tenderness around her newest, youngest son. "We don't find success by avoiding the hard things that come our way."

I wondered what hard things she and Anton had survived.

Vatti S. closed his newspaper to set it aside.

"What seems to be the problem?" he asked, all naiveté and cute.

Our laughter lightened the moment. We had a plan in place in no time.

First up. Fred opened the curtains and the windows. He waved to the assembled. Mobiles and cameras flew into action. He soaked it up as well he should. Handsome. Sexy. Brick shithouse strong. Talented. Soaked through and through. Gunther never had it so good.

Second. Vatti S. played the Lied that ended the first half of the performance in Vienna. With the windows open, the piano wafted softly over the media, the cops, and Rheinhart lurking down the alley.

Third. Fred stepped away from the window with a final wave. He joined Mutti S. at the piano. They sang the first Lied from the second half of Vienna. Muted by the room and the distance and the squeezing of air through curtained windows, the clarity was as Vienna—soft, tender, loving.

Fourth. Hansi called the PR folks for advice and to clarify our plan.

Fifth. I called Restaurant Zecha for advice and suggestions.

Job done. The singing stopped. The piano faded to silence. The windows closed. The curtain softened the noise from the streets. Rheinhart slunk down the alley to disappear out the far end.

We sat quietly, absorbing what happened and ruminating on what was next.

Hansi became master of ceremonies.

Mutti Steiner designated herself as spokesperson. "I am best to take on that Drecker man," she said with resolve, shedding another year or two in her manner.

I stood behind the front door. Hansi brushed his hands through his hair and straightened his shirt collar. Mutti S. pulled on an elegant sweater that had a large broach of a treble clef with a humility of diamonds.

Hansi stepped onto the stoop. Cops stepped forward into the crowd, that now included locals, some wanting the distraction gone from their otherwise quiet street.

'Herr Wortmann' started again from all angles.

"Meine Damen und Herren," he said softly enough that they had to shut up, "Frau Katarin Steiner und Herr Frederic Gluck are delighted with your interest in their performance in Vienna, of which you heard a few selections moments ago. In the spirit of your interest Frau Steiner and Herr Gluck are happy to take your questions and provide answers to the best of their abilities. They request that you pool your questions and select one media representative and one still photographer. In one hour, we will invite your two representatives into Herr und Frau Steiner's home for a one-hour interview and photo opportunity. For those of you waiting outside and for our local Polizei, we have secured an al fresco lunch provided by our good friends from Restaurant Zecha. Again, in one hour I will greet your selected representatives. In the meantime, Frau Steiner has a word."

Mutti S. stepped onto the stoop. Hansi stood by her side, beaming.

"Frau Steiner," the media started again.

Hansi raised his hand and in a martial way quieted them without a word. "Frau Steiner, bitte," he said.

"As Herr Wortmann said, we thank you for your interest in our small recital in Vienna. Herr Steiner and I are grateful that you remember us with such fondness. Given your response and the support of the people of Salzburg, we have secured a venue so that Herr Frederic Gluck, Herr Anton Steiner and I can repeat and perhaps improve upon the recital we shared with our Viennese audience. I am also pleased to announce that Fräulein Margarette Horner will feature in the first half of the recital for an incomparable evening of song and celebration of Salzburg performing arts. We thank the Andreas Steiner and Thomas

McCormack Fund and the Samuel Scott Greyling and Hans Stepan Wortmann Fund for the Digital and Performing Arts for their invaluable support. Further announcements will be forthcoming."

Someone, possibly a neighbor, probably not a cop or a Gunther stooge, applauded. The media folks, flummoxed and unprepared, joined in the applause.

Hansi raised his hand.

Silence.

"Frau Katarin Steiner has a small gift for you."

He stepped off the stoop, standing to the ready.

A note sounded from the piano in the house.

Her a cappella aria from Mozart's *The Magic Flute*, grounding her in her home city and challenging any usurpers to her status, was over in three minutes. The door closed on the stunned crowd. Only after she caught her breath in the arms of Anton did the applause outside rattle the windows.

"I'll bet Gunter heard that from here," Fred said, rubbing Katarin's back and glowing with respect and honor for the gallantry of her singing.

She said, "I'll bet Drecker isn't ready for what comes next."

We focused on questions the media might toss at Mutti S. and Fred, and maybe Vatti S. Halfway through our prep the food van arrived and opened for business, followed closely by a rap on the door, almost polite.

Hansi and I rose to the summons.

"Do you have a permit for this," a studly, handsome cop said in a robotic tone.

"It's rather spontaneous, officer," Hansi said.

"You need a permit to distribute food."

"Yes. That makes sense," I said. "You look like one of the officers who was here when I arrived, over an hour ago."

"Ja, so—."

"I was thinking you saw how this developed. And, well, time to get a permit wasn't available to us."

"Did you try?"

"Have you spoken with Herr Zecha? The owner of the van. He must know how this works."

"You hired him. You are responsible."

Hansi returned to the fray, "What can we do to make this right, officer? Have you had lunch?"

"That would constitute a bribe of a public official."

"Indeed." Hansi paused, looked at me, and went direct. "Is there a ticket for the infraction? A fine? Will we have to go to court?"

The officer looked around to see his partner taking a plate of food. He turned back.

"If you promise no further disturbances, I may let you off with a warning."

"We promise," we said.

"You seem like solid citizens and agreeable gentlemen. I'll have to write this up as a disturbance of the peace."

"Fine, officer. Thank you."

"I'll slip it through your postal slot." He lifted his hat and ran his hand through two people's quantity of hair. He smiled. "My phone number will be on the notice. In case you have any questions—or concerns that I might assist with—with any matter. Not just of this sort. Day or night. Happy to assist." He backed away replacing his hat.

Hansi went back inside.

I meandered over to the food van asking for Herr Zecha. I turned to survey our local Polizei and watched the hairy-headed one berate his colleague for taking a bribe of just below Michelin star quality.

"Herr Greyling, we meet again."

I turned.

Rheinhart.

Fuck.

"You are a busy lad today, my friend. Is your father around?"

"Would you like your meal now or am I to serve you in the Steiners as planned?"

He held my gaze.

"Might be a bit awkward out here. It would be ever so nice to dine inside."

"As you wish, Herr Greyling."

"Shall we say ten minutes?"

"As you wish, Herr Greyling."

I couldn't tell if he was being sarcastic, diplomatic, or prissy. He was a master class in neutrality.

I took a plate of food to the borderline irksome young man in blue. He was startled but politely accepted it as his older partner talked about how he'd always wanted to dine at Restaurant Zecha. We never got our warning.

I asked Rheinhart to join us. He dismissed his crew and driver saying he'd walk back, and would they please inform Herr Zecha that he would be late for prep today.

His charm started with plating the Steiners' servings. He avoided Fred. He asked if he could assist Hansi. He avoided me but sat next to me at table.

"Please tell your father that we are most appreciative of his assisting the media today." Frau Steiner offered a toast of wine from their own cellar.

"You paid for it, so sure, I'll tell him."

"Be rude to my wife again, Herr Zecha, and you will rue the day."

"I already do, Herr Steiner. My apologies, Frau Steiner. I was raised better."

"Indeed," Mutti S. said. Still holding her wine glass, she continued. "Your father tells me you once had a dream, a hope, a desire you shared with him a year ago."

We waited, wondering where this would go.

Rheinhart said, "Dreams die. Desires fade. Hope is, well, not so helpful, in my case."

I put my hand on his arm.

"Herr Greyling is very familiar with the death of dreams and hope." He turned to me. "Are you not, Sam?"

Herr Steiner stood, "Be rude to my son again, Herr Zecha, and you will rue that day as well." He shook his head at Katarin who demurred in reply. He left for the kitchen to pick at the remaining food.

"You have every right to your feelings about me, Rheinhart," I said before anyone else could jump in, which I assumed they would because Herr Steiner declared in public that I am his son.

Mutti S. resumed, "After some debate, Rheinhart, we offer you one year of tuition at Le Cordon Blue Paris. One year of tuition will gain you access to culinary, wine, management, and marketing courses of study. Was this not your dream?"

Stunned silence.

Vatti S. returned to his place, licking his fingers. Katarin slapped his hands and offered her serviette. He said, "Young man, you must commit to one full year. We will do our best to find you lodgings. Your father will assist with living and travel expenses. One caveat, to get that on the table immediately, is that you may not use Herr Drecker's assistance and once you leave Salzburg for Paris you are not to interact with him or his emissaries in any way. Other than that, you are free to be a young man in Paris. How fortunate is that?"

Stunned silence.

Rheinhart stood, impeccably straight. "I am pleased my father was able to provide sustenance to the media to help cover your contempt for a friend of mine. Herr und Frau Steiner, thank you for your hospitality and offer. Fred, I wish you all the best.

Hans, you don't know what you are up against. Herr Greyling, go home. Leave Austria to Austrians. We don't deserve your kind."

He was gentle in closing the door behind him.

"He has six months to decide," said Vatti S., "and will need years to grow up."

Fred turned domestique to remove remaining plates, glasses, and utensils.

"Mutti und Vatti," said Hansi, "you can't afford to send him to Le Cordon Bleu in Paris or any other city in the world. When did you come up with that?"

Mutti retorted, "Never you mind, Hans, it will all work out."

"He's too smitten with Drecker," said Fred dropping onto the sofa next to me.

"I wanted to ask you, Frederic," said Mutti, "how did you have the courage to extract yourself from that Gunther fellow?"

Fair question. We waited. Fred pondered.

"I trusted you cared about what I want to do." He pursed his lips and nodded confidence.

"That is what we are offering this young man," Mutti said. "He will come around if none of us breaks the chain of trust that is being built. An offer such as Le Cordon Bleu is the foundation. Making that happen is one step on his journey."

"Changing the subject," said Hansi, with a chuckled mood lightener, "he nailed you, Sam. Go home, Uncle Sam. You aren't Austrian, Uncle Sam. Ooooo. That must have hurt." He reached over to tousle my hair. Fred joined in from his side.

"If you boys break anything you will pay a price," laughed Vatti S.

When the tickling and tousling stopped, I re-sheveled myself, hair and clothes in place, a grin planted, Piccaso-like. I turned too pensive for the nattering ambience.

"Rheinhart is right. I am not Austrian and will never be. I am an outsider and will always be. That doesn't mean I don't have a place or a stake in Salzburg or this country. I will probably never understand the culture or the humor or some of the food choices you all make. Doesn't mean I can't engage with the culture, indulge the humor, and tolerate the food. As Mutti says, it will all work out."

"Oooo, Uncle Sam goes dark and brooding," Hansi half whispered.

Mutti filtered what I said through her wisdom sieve, "Perhaps your reasoning is a way to help Rheinhart see that narrowing options for a short while will expand his options for his future. I think a nudge from Uncle Sam might do the trick."

Another firm knock on the door.

"Shit," said Hansi, "the interview."

Muttis S. said, "Hans Wortmann, do not let me hear that language in this house."

"I bet you forgot, too, Mutti."

"I had hoped *they* would forget." She smiled.

An hour later, after staged photos and too many questions about the tiff with Gunther, and after Mutti S. turned those questions into the perfect PR we had intended, and after Fred wobbled at first then stood his ground again, we ushered the reporter and photographer out onto the street.

We all had smug and satisfied looks about us.

"Time will tell," I said.

Mutti S. pulled Anton to his feet in one great swoosh of energy, and strode to the music room. "Time for practice, Herr Gluck." She smiled back at the three of us on the sofa.

One or two desperate young media types loitered against the wall of the house opposite. The cops had shifted to the end of the street, both looking back at us. We waved but got no response. One of the reporters, or social influencers, half-heartedly shouted, "Herr Wortmann, a word please."

"Announcements forthcoming," he twirled around to shout then threw his arm around my neck.

"Katarin has me on a mission," I said.

"It can wait until you return. You have yet to change your flights."

"I'll meet you back at Getreidegasse. You have more calls to make, meiner Herz."

We stopped at the bridge to share a culturally and socially acceptable public Le Cordon Bleu in Paris type kiss. Before I could wipe his saliva off my face, he was on his phone.

I loped toward the Steingasse hoping Rheinhart hadn't returned to Restaurant Zecha to tell his father to stay the fuck out of his life.

Eighteen

Being early afternoon mid-week, an older than me couple snogged in the corner booth, the bartender fiddled with the sound system, and I ordered my usual but I didn't have history with this not-Fred so I had to order my two-finger single malt neat.

I sat in my usual place nursing my drink, which arrived with a side of mixed nuts. Rheinhart was nowhere to be seen. I worked on plan B, opening my phone to call the airline.

I hadn't noticed before that the door to the toilet was on the same wall that had been my backstop during several drunken outings and oglings of Fred's promise of high-quality service.

The privy door flashed open. It would have struck me except for the strategically hung rubber door stopper attached to my backstop.

Rheinhart pushed the door shut, turning so he didn't see me, then walked toward the exit. His wave to Augustus – the bartender had a name nearly as sexy as Frederic – was dejection, defeat.

"Hey, Austrian!" I shouted, a tad too loud, because the older-than-me couple glanced my way as Rheinhart turned.

"Augustus, bring the man his favorite," I stood, ready to greet my friend. My need to take care of puppies tingled in my chest. My brain farted caution and compassion. I wondered if this had been a good choice or if Hansi's suggestion had been the better route. Too late. I was in it now.

"American empire. This is what it's like. Being stalked in gay toilets and drinking holes. Reaching beyond what propaganda trumpets down into the lives of meagre men to wrench them from family, friends, and home." His elegance and cogent thinking startled me and took me back to my darkened pub not far down the Gasse, remembering similar debates. I reminded myself that the world changes one conversation at a time.

"I love that youth speaks its mind," I said indicating the stool next to my highchair.

"Too bad no one listens." An edge of depression.

His drink of choice arrived.

"What even is that?" I touched the glass like a great ape exploring human first contact.

"Not for single malt oldies." He drooped his head my way.

"Talk to me," I said.

"Why? You and yours taunt me. Drecker half ignores me because I am not a source of revenue. He calls me a taker that he tolerates and pushes around."

"What does he offer you?"

"He told me once that all he wanted was to be accepted, to belong, to be seen. He said it during one drunken pool party when he lamented you, his great and powerful muse."

I stifled.

"He loved you, you know. Deeply. In his way. When he bares his chest, he can be a kind and thoughtful man. It's when he feels cornered that he does the nasty things he does. Even sad little me can see how lonely and afraid he is."

"You didn't answer my question."

He tapped the glass. Not a sniff or a slight taste of whatever was in it.

"I don't know, Sam. I don't know what he offers or why I seek what I don't know. He's got an authority I can't explain."

"Drugs? Sex? Pretty students."

"I suppose."

He wiped the moisture off the glass, turning it to get all the wet off.

"Sam? Am I like him or am I like you?"

There's a binary choice I hadn't anticipated, worse than black and white. I ignored his politeness of not drinking because he seemed uninterested. I downed a finger.

"You are Rheinhart Zecha. Only you can determine who that is."

"You sound like my dad."

"About the same age."

"You're older. I will never let you forget that." No hint of humor.

"What does your dad say about these things?"

"You know damn good and well that he and Frau Steiner concocted this Paris thing."

"You're feeling coerced?"

"Not exactly. I feel like I have to grow up. I don't want that. Not yet. Look at what growing up did to you." A little humor there, I hoped. "You left your adventure and didn't look back."

"So much looking back. I sometimes forgot that Thomas was in front of me. I don't want that for you, Rheinhart." I took a sip of dark audacity. "Be decisive but not regretful."

"Do you regret?"

"Fucking Jesu Christopherus. Who knows. No. Yes. Yeah, I have lots of regrets. I acknowledge them and say hi as they wriggle through my brain. It took me a long time to not grab onto them and beat the crap out of myself with little more than what are memories."

Was I lying again? These past few weeks challenged my need to prevaricate. I was getting the sense that I might have grown up a bit—finally. Regret and small victories.

"Not to be too clichéd," I ventured.

"Oh god, old man lecture pretending to be wisdom," he chucked half of a chuckle. "Sorry. Go on. I am interested in what you say, Herr Greyling. I don't know why I like you. But there's that, I suppose." He consumed half of his mystery liquid.

"You are a very smart man, Rheinhart. Focus on what gets you what you want. The world will take care of itself."

"That's a weak cliché, Sam Greyling. I expect more."

"I guess I'm not a cliché kinda man."

He threw his head back in a full throttled guffaw—at my expense. If self-deprecation got him out of his funk, then I was happy to take the hit. I joined in.

When he snorted his last, he put his hand on my shoulder and squeezed a masculine tenderness.

"If only Fred hadn't taken your fancy," he said, scooting off his stool. "I must go. I'll brush my teeth before I tell Father my plans. Perhaps you will be in town long enough to know, too."

His flattened, warm hand on my cheek and his rough thumb caressing my lips made me wonder that if Fred hadn't taken my fancy might this charmer have been my holiday fling.

He was walking away but I grabbed his arm and pulled him back into an embrace.

"Don't be a cliché," he said.

I pulled him closer into a long, wet, kiss.

"You will find your way," I said, pushing him away as if a son had kissed his father.

"Impulsive old man," he smiled, tweaking my cheek. "You are wiser than you know, Herr Greyling."

He walked to the exit throwing greetings to Augustus and the couple in the corner.

I finished his unfinished drink. Sweet but sour. Sticky but smooth. I didn't ask Augustus for the recipe. It wasn't unpleasant.

Even though Augustus didn't wink or flirt, I left a hefty Euro note to ensure proper service my next visit. American cliché all the way.

On the way back to Getreidegasse, I poked into the jewelry shop at the cheap end of the passage. I bought the friendship ring I had seen a few days before. I slipped it on. A perfect fit. I hoped it would be perfect for its recipient.

I also stopped at the high-quality shop at the inner end of the passage. I was given a sales tour of men's rings. I took notes in my phone but was not allowed to photograph them. I'd sneak back after-hours to do that through the window. My stealth-self wondered if I would be clichéd enough to do what I was thinking.

The stairwell smelled of dark, Turkish coffee. Hansi was in his reading chair nursing an espresso in a glass cup. He glanced up then finished the sentence, paragraph, or chapter he was savoring, because he devoured what he read like a Michelin-starred meal. His contentment filled the room.

"Progress?" he queried.

I flopped onto the sofa considering what book I should start in order to leave it partly read as another incentive to return.

"Do all retired doctors sit and read?"

"Meditative," he smiled, enfolding the bookmark in place as he closed his tome.

"Rheinhart knows his dilemma," I said. "He nursed it over a drink at the pub. There's a new bartender. Not Fred."

"You sound disappointed."

"It was feeling familiar is all."

"And Rheinhart?"

"We kissed," I looked to check his response.

"We're even, then," he said. "Well, you fucked him and kissed him so that makes you one point up. If we are keeping score."

He joined me on the sofa, leaning into me while hugging one arm to near extinction.

I adjusted to save my arm from amputation and kissed the top of his head.

He fingered the new bauble on my right-hand ring finger, twisting it a few times. "What's this?"

"A ring."

"I've never seen you wear jewelry."

"Haven't since Thomas."

"Why now?" he twisted out of my embrace to look me square on.

"It's a gift for someone." Not sure why I was teasing him, but the game was on. I decided to play it, within the rules.

He didn't want to play. He stood. No particular emotion in that. Maybe he thought the ring was for him, so he played coy, receding to the kitchen. He shouted back, "You hungry? I got some things to munch on before dinner."

He was startled to see me in the doorway.

"I need a nap," I said, unbuttoning my tourist apparel one sexy twist at a time.

He leaned against the counter. Smirk. Smirk. Smirk.

"What will I taste in your mouth?" he said. A question I had never been asked before. Thomas would urge me toward a mouthwash every time we got randy, which told me he didn't want to taste much at all.

Hansi didn't need to undress. Sex oozed through his shirt and trousers. He taught the fabrics how to shout his desire. The drape of his tension, of his hint of movement, of his happiness, enticed me against him.

"Sex sommelier will have to discern my taste in detail." I slid my tongue around his neck, up to his ear, then to his mouth which eagerly accepted me.

"Hints of malt. Overtones of Zecha. And, ick, some sticky substance. What have you been drinking?"

We laughed our way to the bed, not bothering to close the curtains. If someone up on the Monchsberg wanted to watch, bring it on.

He fucked me like he had years before. He made sure I knew he had fucked me. He made sure the taste in my mouth was of him. He made sure I would remember him for as long as it takes for me to return. He told me that as he shot his wad into me. For the second time.

"You better fucking come back, Greyling," he said, sliding off my sweaty body.

We wrapped around each other. His breath returning to normal. Mine still as rapid as my heart rate.

"You don't believe me," I said licking his neck.

"There's a history."

"There's a Trust to which my name is firmly attached."

"You said yourself that you can manage things from the States."

"Yeah. We can chat on any number of streaming services, too. Or talk by phone. Or write letters. Or send pigeons." I started to unwrap.

"No. Not yet." He held me in a Wortmann vice grip.

"Trust means letting go," I pushed away.

"You are so predictable." I could tell he wanted to laugh. He moved to his side of the bed, arranging the pillows.

"I think the word you have been seeking all these decades is cliché d."

"Tri lingual now. Thanks for the French lesson." He was no longer on the precipice of humor.

"Hansi," I stayed on my side. I reached out to touch him, running my hand over his washboard along his trail stopping short of his junk. I twisted his pubes. He reached down to stop me.

"Don't hurt me, Greyling." The word 'again' hung between us.

I moved back to the other side of the bed, mirroring his pillow and arms.

We contemplated the ceiling, light slowly moving across it, the beveled glass squares at the top creating a flowing, Salzach River impression. I thought about the log. Stuck.

"I am asking you to believe me." That flowed around the stuck.

I waited for a reply. I turned toward him. He had fallen asleep, sex countering the effect of an espresso in a lovely glass cup.

"I am coming back to marry you, Hans Stepan Wortmann," I whispered.

Nineteen

He gave no hint of having heard me.

Through our hour-long nap, through our shower, and through dinner at the Greek place, he didn't hint of any comprehension of my whisper.

Finishing our usual desserts, we got a call from Anders that the paperwork had been processed by the state government in record time because he knew someone who knew another someone who knew a higher up someone who promulgated the acceptance.

We ordered ouzo to celebrate.

On the way to the river, he pushed me against the wall, "I need to clean your palate. I want every last taste of ouzo out of you."

"The ouzo is gone but the happiness remains," I said, using a memory from my student days as a cliché or reassurance or a grounding in the giddiness I was feeling. Ouzo bares all. Ouzo doesn't mix with wine all that well. We meandered on each sidewalk to the river. We sat as lovers on our bench. Me leaning against his chest and neck. His arm around my shoulders. We faced into the city of salt, waiting for the lights.

"I want to see Mutti Wortmann before I leave."

"She will like that."

"How is her health?"

"She'll be here when you return."

The lights started popping on. We oohed and aahed with the rest of the tourists hanging about and across the river.

"About that," I said.

"Predictable." He shook me harder than I suspected he might want to. I nestled back into him without comment. "How many times am I going to fuck you so I know you will return?"

"What I was going to say," my elbow poke hit lower than his gut, although he didn't say anything through his intake of air, "I think you need to go ahead with recitals, Trust planning, and whatever Gunther throws at us. We can stream when you need me."

"Was that what you were going to say?"

I sat up, twined my arms around his neck.

A young couple biking by laughed.

"Wait until you are my age," I yelled after them. "You'll be happy you waited." I dropped the shout.

"Hansi, barring some disaster, I am coming back."

"Your first caveat," he said, turning to look across to Mirabel Palace.

"That's not fair," I pushed off him to sit with head in hands.

"There's history," he said.

"You keep reminding."

He rubbed my back. His massaging warmed my muscles, relaxing my spine and my neck. I lolled my head.

"Will you marry me?"

Perfect timing with the lights on the castle blaring on. The crescendo of the tourist whoops and hollers filled in for bells and whistles.

We looked at each other for the longest time.

We had said it at the same time.

We also said at the same time. Him: "Are you playing games?" Me: "Is this a ploy?"

We knew neither was true but speaking makes fear visible.

Our smiles trembled into laughter.

"Yes!" We said at the same time.

"Come with me," I said, "I have something for you."

At the top of Getreidegasse, he inserted his key.

"No." I grabbed him from behind and turned him to walk further, "You think you know clichés? Hold tight, mein Herz."

The shop keeper looked a little confused when I said I wanted to purchase two of the same men's rings she had shown me before. She looked from me to Hansi and back. I turned to Hansi.

"Predictable?" I said.

"You are, yes." He nodded to the shopkeeper.

She reached beneath the display and then handed him a gold box with black lettering.

He flipped it open.

Two identical rings shone in the LED lights. The sparkle of single diamonds nestled in white gold lit up the room and the space between us.

"You fell into my trap. It took a while, though. I ordered these a week ago. Frau Treicher got your measurements the other evening. You are so predictable."

"How did you know this style was—." He put a finger to my lips.

"She saw you from the back, eyeing that row of rings, which happened to be the ones I liked, too. She knew because I used to stop by to gaze at them before you showed up at Augies that first afternoon."

"She doesn't know me from Adam." I looked at her and she demurred into a shy grin, cheeks full of mischief.

"Phones have photos," he smiled.

I kissed him. He pulled back.

"Let's see if these things fit."

Frau Treicher applauded with her fingers and palms in a lady-like manner.

On our walk to what was now our bar to celebrate, another choice I'd made as a student assaulted my memory.

Twenty

Back in the day, Herr Geist, our student group's erstwhile travel agent extraordinaire and all-round entrepreneur, looking to get a quick Schilling or one hundred, shook my hand and directed me out of his office. I was there to negotiate a group trip to Budapest, or at least get the skeleton of it started so a quote could be sent to our onsite adult director. On the way out to the street we stopped at a desk of one of his agents.

"Herr Greyling, Herr Drecker will be the point person on specifics and your contact when I am not available. Gunther, please be sure Sam and his group are well looked after." Geist turned and walked away.

Gunther stood and bowed like an 18th century Austrian high prince.

Not knowing Austrian protocol, I extended my hand for a shake. "I hope you will help me through the intricacies of details and languages," I said.

"All will be perfect, Herr Greyling."

"Sam. Call me Sam."

"Wunderbar. Gunther," he bowed again.

I absented myself to the street because it was all a bit weird. Amiable, I supposed. But weird.

That evening I bolted out the door of the Center, late for dinner. I ran into a short, stuffy wall of a man. I excused myself and darted around him.

"Herr Greyling," the stout one called after me, "I have a draft itinerary if you would like to review it."

I sent my friends ahead and bounced back.

"I'm sorry, I—?" I stuttered an apology.

"Gunther. Drecker. Travel agent with Herr Geist?"

"Right. I'm—late for dinner. I have an hour between classes tomorrow. Can we do this then?"

"We need to book hotels." He winced, as if I might yell at him.

"I'll be at your office at 2:15 p.m. I hope that works."

I turned and ran after my friends. At the intersection, I looked back. Gunther stood with the papers still dangling in front of him, a look of consternation pouting out of him. I waved. He dropped the papers to his side.

Shortly before the trip I was at the travel agents' reviewing final details with our bus driver and group director. As we were leaving, Gunther asked if he could speak to me. The others left. He pulled me close to the door in a conspiratorial huddle of two.

"Sam?" His mousy tone was hard to hear with a teletype going and phones ringing. "Sam, would you have a drink with me after work? We can go to wherever you want. I will buy, of course, because I am inviting you." His half smile echoed his mousy looks.

"Gunter. Yeah. Unexpected. Uh. Sure, why not. How about after we get back from Budapest. I can stop by and set something up."

"I was thinking tonight. I know a pub at the end of Steingasse. No one goes there. It would be private."

I go there, I didn't say out loud. I wanted to bop him on the head and scream at him. I had also never seen him there, but I wasn't there 24/7 or anything more than Friday nights.

"Meet me there after work." I said. "There will be others. You might know them. This is a small town." I tried to laugh it off and hoped he'd turn the offer down and I could pretend this interaction never happened. If nothing else, a group of guys would offer a buffer of sorts. I darted out the door into a soft rain—refreshing, cleansing, and freeing.

Racing back to the Center for an art history lecture with slides and constant commentary, I forgot about my 'date' with the junior travel agent. I spent most of the lecture wondering how Hansi would look if naked as Apollo, buffed as the Discus Thrower, and as sexy as Narcissus, although I hoped for more attention on me than his own reflection. Test on Tuesday rang through me at dinner and my solo walk to the pub, anticipation building that Hansi had trained in from Innsbruck for the weekend.

He didn't. Unless he caught a late train, he wasn't there waiting for me as had happened most weekends. Leon wasn't there either.

There was a mousy man in our cubby hole. I eyed him while ordering my liter of bier and large pretzel. I looked around for another table because I wasn't in the mood for meeting new guys, especially the mice of Salzburg. No options that I could see.

I shuffled to the cubby. Uncertain. Incurious. Offended someone would take a table that was my usual spot.

As I approached, he turned. I moaned. The 'date' was on time, or early, or late, or—there. After work was unspecific. Shit. Shit. Shit.

"I thought you weren't coming."

"Delayed. Group things. American students being dumb."

He brightened. "You're here now. Please sit. I thought this table was out of the way and no one would bother us. I'm not used to this sort of place."

Fuck. Fuck. Fuck. A closeted travel agent. What did I know.

I sat as far opposite as I could get. He scooched nearer.

Please, dear god – I hid my plea as deep behind my eyes as I could muster without crossing them – bring Leon and Hansi as fast as you can.

Gunther told me about his family. He told me about his work. He told me he thought Herr Geist was the best way to learn about the travel industry. He told me about all the tours he'd created for their small company and how he thought he could open more agencies if Herr Geist would let him. He told me how committed he was to being successful and important, and that people would know his name far and wide.

Please dear god, what have you done to them. Did you derail a train? Did you take them off this earth? What have you done, dear god? I prayed like I hadn't since I was an altar boy. I begged god to end this. I reminded god that he could never send me to hell because I was living it—in my pub no less, surrounded by gay men, drinking for fuck sake, fornicating upstairs for the life of the virgin. I reminded god that if he didn't send Hansi and Leon or anyone else on the planet, I would never speak like this to him again.

"Sam? Are you OK?"

Gunther touched my hand.

I slunk up from the depths of perdition to see him approximating compassion. He squeezed my hand. Tender. Soft. Controlling.

"Sorry, Gunther, I've had a long week with classes and planning Budapest, and I don't know." I shook my head to stop the flames of god's non-response. "I'm really tired. I need to call it a night."

"I haven't heard about you, Sam. I want to know everything." Enthusiasm. Intrigue. Control.

I looked at my watch. Three hours before I would normally leave inebriated and needing to pee, stumbling to the alley to add to the flow of Salzburg's underbelly of smells and sounds.

"It's getting late. Don't you work tomorrow?"

"So kind of you, Sam. Yes, I do. We open at 10:00 a.m. We could have breakfast before. Or supper after. I like you, Sam. I want to be friends."

"Let's see how it develops," I said. Coward. Escaping. Cursing god.

"I'll walk you back," he said.

"Oh." Cornered. "No need. I have an art assignment due on Monday and I have to report on things about Salzburg that inspire me at night." Where did that come from. Was this my defense? A lie. A fabrication to cover what I should have said and that would put a stop to what was coming. I was resorting to lying to cover my fear and loathing.

"I can help. I plan tours for American tourists. Where do you need to go?"

Crap. Crap. Crap.

"You know, Gunther, I think that can wait. I am very tired. I'll go right to my room and call it a night."

"I'll walk you back. It's kind of on my way. I shouldn't be out much later anyway. Mother and Father, you know."

We clambered out of the cubby hole. I said good night to the bartender. He looked at me like I was abandoning him and why wasn't I staying until closing time like usual. I shrugged and discreetly pointed. He nodded either understanding or encouragement. He thought I'd hooked up with Gunther. I didn't want that reaching the ears of either Hansi or Leon. Walk of embarrassment.

Out on the Steingasse we had our first tiff. I didn't know it would be the first of several.

"You aren't interested in me, are you, Sam?"

Stuck.

Lie.

"We're getting to know each other, Gunther. It all takes time." I turned to walk away.

He grabbed my arm too hard for the occasion, "Don't be like the others, Sam. I won't allow it. I like you, Sam. I can show you a good time. I get travel vouchers to Venice, Rome, West Berlin. I could take you to Monaco."

I twisted free.

Lie.

"That sounds great, Gunther. Like I said, let's talk about that down the road."

"You didn't say that Sam. Don't ever lie to me, Sam. It is unbecoming of you."

"Gunther." Firm. Direct. Not a lie. "If you want to be my friend then you need to respect my boundaries. I want to go home. By myself."

"You are like all the rest."

"I doubt that Gunther, but if you say so." I turned to find my alley because I was not going back into the pub for the bartender to see that walk of shame and have him laugh at me. I had my dignity, too, for god's sake, even though I was no longer talking to that myth in the sky.

We parted.

"Regret reveals itself in many ways, Sam." His mousy voice bounced the length of Steingasse. I ducked into the alley to avoid its reverberations in my head, if not off the close buildings and cobbled stones.

I couldn't go to my room. That would be overly sad.

Rather than cutting through Altstadt, I look the long way on this side of the Salzach to the footbridge that took me to Augies. Not my usual Friday routine, I stalked around looking for familiar faces. I found a subset of our group playing a game of flipping bierdeckeln, seeing who could flip and catch the most. They folded me into the play and drinking.

All I could think about was Hansi and why he didn't save me from that Gunther fellow.

Twenty-One

Herr Steiner and Fred were more interested in the articles they found in print and electronic press. Fred relished showing Vatti S. the wiles of social media. Vatti recoiled to the four or five print media he bought at the local newsstand.

Mutti S. sat at the dining table planning the Salzburg repeat recital. With the hype growing she pondered if the size of the venue was big enough or should it remain intimate to stoke the clamor for more. Something to be said about supply creating demand.

"You aren't going on the road," Hansi reminded her.

"We can get people to come to Salzburg."

"How much do you want to be doing this? You did retire."

I let the family tussle it through.

"Cher came out of retirement many times."

I had to jump in, "You follow Cher? Mutti Steiner?"

"Follow is not the right word, Sam. Perhaps 'aware' is the better word. Her songs are quite lovely and full-on, as Anders warns me when he catches me listening to her."

"Still," Hansi said, "you aren't Cher."

"We are nearly the same age." She tipped her head to a make point.

"She has people. You have us. A bit of a difference."

I laughed. "That makes me a performer's 'people.' With Fred thrust onto the stage of life I might end up being a roadie." He wasn't staying local for long.

Vatti S. stuck his head around the corner.

"You able to practice today, Schatzi?"

She tested with a warmup, not leaving her tasks. Listening to her doing scales was a recital unto itself.

"I think in thirty minutes, Herzi."

Hansi poked my arm "Let's go for a walk. There's a new installation at the Contemporary. I'll buy lunch."

We hoofed it across the bridge.

The installation was a pile of newspapers flowing out of and crumpled against a large trash bin, creating a floor swallowing labyrinth starting in an ancient rune and ending in a vagina. We knew this because we read the artist's statement and description. We also noticed the artist was male.

"If you have to describe it then it isn't working," I said, too smug and too distracted by the sound I was hearing coming from the bowels of the museum.

Hansi grabbed me. "Let's get out before we have to dumpster dive."

We darted down the concrete stairwell, flew through the doors, and parked ourselves among the tourists facing our view over the city.

Gunther's voice erupted through the doors. Tourists looked around in disbelief. They moved away from the patio in waves as the volume grew closer.

"Let's hike the Monchsberg." I grabbed Hansi and walked toward the lightly forested path.

"Well." Thrown at us like a lasso toward cattle. "If it isn't the crème de la crème of Salzburg society." He made a barely softer aside to his much smaller gaggle of brunettes, nary a blond in the bunch. "The nouveau are so easy to discern in a crowd. They slink around without poise or dignity."

We stood alone against the Dreckernaut.

"Hello, Gunter. What a pleasure," I said.

"Lies," he shot back, tweaking his single earring, the new rage of the nouveau riche of Paris and Milan. It would seem.

"Not again," I false whined. "I will learn one day, Herr Drecker."

Hansi added, "Want to join us on a small hike around this lovely Berg?" He pointed toward the trail head.

"Ha. Nature. I admire it from afar. It is too tiring to engage." He examined his nails. "Have you launched into hosting visual artists, too?"

"We could not possibly compete with your exemplary knowledge and passion," I said. I tried to turn Hansi toward the forest. He stood fast.

He stepped close to Gunther.

"You have so many good qualities," he said sniffing in Gunther's face, "it is a tragedy that you hide them behind your personal shame and fear. You could be agreeable, and perhaps even likeable, if you'd drop the pretense. Just a thought."

"Hrmpf." Encased in a pitched squeal was the reply. If Gunther was a happy man, or even content with what he'd gained in life, the noise would have been of glee. Instead, it was sarcasm nearly as thick as his makeup, clownish in the daylight.

"If you think I regret my life you are mistaken. I would not have this," he swept his arm across Altstadt and beyond, "without knowledge and passion, and a fucking lot of hard work. My empire is earned. No recital is going to stop that. No Trust or fancy Fund will interfere. You," his nose and arm thrust our direction, "will not upend this." He swept his tiring arm down his person then pointed at the castle at the other end of Monchsberg. "That is my stay and anchor. The strength of centuries grounds me in my mission."

He stood wrapped in himself.

His brunettes waited.

We turned to leave.

"Leaving so soon," he said. Almost sad. Almost inviting us to drop an anchor.

"Nothing here for us. We saw the new installation and now we need to cleanse our eyes," Hansi might not have wanted to sound so harsh and mocking. What did I know.

"He will be a mighty force in the annals of the visual arts," Gunther unwound, looked at the benches, and determined that only the common people sat on furniture that unclean.

"We wish you well, Gunther," I said tugging on Hansi's arm.

"Hansel and Gretel without breadcrumbs. Tragic."

I tugged harder on Hansi's body. He was tense. "Don't go where I think you are thinking of going," I whispered. "Oh look, a red squirrel," I pointed at a moving animal among the fallen pine needles.

"Stop!" A shout from behind Gunther.

The assembled complied.

Rheinhart stepped from the far side of the overlook.

"This is all leftover crap from years ago. Shame on you. It isn't fun to watch—anymore." He stepped around Gunther who clutched his breasts with both hands. The gaggle shrank onto benches like rows of tattling children.

"You two," he shot us a look of death, "have made your point. Salzburg knows you and the Steiners are a force now. What else do you need to do?"

He turned on Gunther. "You are a caricature. The whole country knows your game. This is so unbecoming of what you could be. No one likes you, Gunther, because you are phony and absurd. No one can see what good you are trying to do because you are clumsy and rude. All of you need to grow up." He looked at me. "Sam, make up your fucking mind and get a life. You mope around like a child without a toy." Switching to Hans. "Hans, Andreas is dead. That's it for you. He's dead. If Sam doesn't come back, fuck him. There are others."

He turned toward the city.

"And you," Hansi said, "what about Rheinhart? Staying stuck here or moving on?"

Rheinhart turned to Gunther.

"I am going to Paris, Herr Drecker. I have a gift in hand. I plan to become more than you have offered me." He stood firm.

"I have offered you nothing, Herr Zecha. You hang about looking for crumbs like a squirrel in the forest." He flicked a finger toward Rheinhart, and probably Hansi and me.

"You cannot stop hurting people, Gunther." Rheinhardt continued. "More's the pity because you have a great responsibility but use it with contempt. You are the sad one among us. I hope you see yourself for what you have become— a caricature of loneliness."

"You are banished, Herr Zecha. Never to grace the likes of me again."

Rheinhart walked past us. He whispered, "I need to talk to you." He nearly skipped onto the path, scaring the squirrel off another direction.

"Goodbye, Gunther," I said with a wave. "I won't see you for a while."

"Indeed," he said with a swish of a turn into the museum.

We marched along the path in silence, reaching an open meadow that faced toward the Untersberg. We snuggled into the long grass, damp seeping through our trousers.

"Going to Paris." I set the statement among the weeds.

Rheinhart tore grasses from their stems. He twisted them into a rope and smacked it against his legs.

"Vatti wants me to assure him I'll come back to Salzburg. I told him I might not. We had a row. I left just before we opened. I didn't go back. I don't know why I am so angry."

He looked lost.

"I don't know if I want this. Paris. Le Cordon Bleu. My whole life in a kitchen."

Was his sadness an invitation to chuck my thoughts at him?

Hansi charged in. "What do you want from us? We'll help if we can."

"I know I teased you, Sam, about not coming back and then showing up."

"That was teasing?" I chuckled to lighten the mood.

"Were you afraid to come back, Sam? I think I am afraid to leave."

"The other side of fear is freedom." I surprised myself with a hint of wisdom.

Rheinhart shifted his weight and tossed his grass whip down the hill.

"I've never been to Paris. I don't speak French. I'm not sure I like their food."

"We can get you a tutor here, so you have some rudimentary sense of the language. Mutti and Vatti Steiner will introduce you to Austrians living there. People come from all over the world to study there. In a short time, you'll have friends."

"I don't have friends here."

"What? In the pub I see you glad handing and hugging and kissing any man that moves. You've got friends."

"You guys know me better than they do."

"Then you've got friends."

"What if I don't like it? What if I fail?"

"You are approaching this like a death sentence," Hansi continued. "All it is, is an opportunity. A chance to explore an option. Le Cordon Bleu isn't your life. It is a steppingstone to something yet to be found."

Rheinhart stretched his legs long and lithe and leaned back on his elbows. Wisps of cloud langered over us. A siren sounded below. Bells, marking the time, rang proud. We waited.

"Can I go with you to America?"

"You won't like the food," I said.

Hansi took the serious route. "To what end? Seems like you are avoiding what is a great option. Rheinhart, it will be a great time. People don't spend 24 hours a day in a kitchen. Paris is fantastic. Full of the passions of youth."

"And a fantastic club scene, gay neighborhood, and partying." My great international knowledge focused on the important stuff.

"Am I being stupid?" he asked.

"Yes," we both said.

"There's that—." His response shouted despondence.

"If you don't like it you can leave."

"The Steiners want a year commitment."

"They have their hands full with Fred," Hansi said, implying the tribulations of Gunther in that brief sentence. "If you come back, I'll deal with their aspirations."

I ratcheted up the pressure, like the damp seeping into my butt crack, "What will you do if you don't do this?"

"No idea," he said, shame and self-doubt welling in his eyes.

"Then you have nothing to lose," I said.

I marveled that midday heat could create such localized humidity by raising the dank and damp high enough off the ground that a small micro-cloud floated around us. I waited for rainbows and unicorns. Alas. Not even a red squirrel.

"Vatti wanted an answer by noon. I'm late." He stood, shook both of our hands, and walked away with wet spots on his shirt and trousers. We held our snarky jokes until he was out of sight and out of ear shot. The bells of Salzburg pealed the one o'clock hour.

"Don't laugh at him. We will look much worse when we stand up," I said.

Hansi rolled on top of me.

"You'll look worse because you, mein Schatz, are going to soak up a lake worth of water while I lay on top of you to allow the sun to dry me out."

He kissed me. I welcomed his tongue into my mouth.

I talked around it. "Maybe Fred can help him see it for the better."

"What?" Hansi pulled back.

I repeated.

"Good idea. Let's take him to dinner at Zecha and have a chat."

"Two nights of fine dining in a week. That will be fun."

I inserted my tongue to stop him talking more. I ran my hands over his back, down to his butt. He was dryer than me. Before he could dry completely, I pushed him off, stood, and turned round and round to see how wet I was. Perhaps if I plunged into the horse fountain at the entrance to the tunnel, I would have a better story to tell.

We walked over to the castle, down the service road, and back to Getreidegasse.

Hansi phoned Zecha for a reservation at 8:00 p.m.

We stripped naked and hung our clothes to dry.

The bed coverings needed rearranging. We obliged with an hour of fucking, sucking, tasting, and laughing.

We headed to the Steiners to see if Fred was free for dinner.

Twenty-Two

Hansi's kiss and fondling my crotch startled me awake.

"What the fuck?" I muttered a complicated dream into the reaches of never-to-remember because it was weird.

"We gotta get going. Busy day. Come on, get that thing taken care of and move it." He tweaked his head toward my stiffy.

"What happened last night?" Stiffy slumped.

"Fred was great. Rheinhart's going to Paris. We are paying for Fred to accompany him by train. We gotta get Mutti to arrange a one-day training for him with someone from l'Opera. She'll love doing that."

I rolled to the side of the bed. Stiffy gone.

"Aren't we going to forest Castle Wortmann?"

"That's why you gotta get moving, mein Schatz."

He had two boiled eggs, pastries, juice, and coffee ready to scarf and we were out the door five minutes after I brushed my teeth.

I knocked on Mutti W's door later than planned. Hansi went to the administrator's office to review papers and speak with the head nurse and doctor—a scheduled quarterly review.

"Sam, my American son, come, come, come," she welcomed me to her bosom, purring like a kitten, soft and warm, but a bit pitchy.

"Hans will be here shortly. Paperwork." I disembarked from her hug.

She pulled me into the kitchenette in the open plan of her apartment. We stood on the linoleum pretending to make coffee.

"That man is here again. Out there." She nodded toward the patio. "I asked him to leave but he didn't."

I turned to see Gunther either enjoying nature or abhorring his life. His back to us.

"You sit down and have your coffee. I'll speak with that man." I walked her to her chair and patted her throw around her legs.

"Gunther," I said, closing the door, joining him to look across the lawn to the forest. "Why are you here?"

"It is not you to whom I wish to speak." He turned his head to look at the wall separating this patio from the neighbor's.

"Oh. OK. I'll leave you to it." I walked back to the door.

"However, since you are here." He turned to face me or to rebuke nature. I wasn't sure which because for the first time I saw him without at least one layer of makeup.

I held my scrutiny and mild shock in place.

"I never liked you, Sam Greyling. I never liked a thing about you." He sauntered to a chair and rested his hand, sans jewels, on the back. "I used you because I was in love with Hans."

He seemed to want me to laugh or object or scream or react.

"I knew you would be leaving at the end of your school year. I waited until you were gone. It was difficult being around you, you know." He paused. "You beguiled Hans. He would have come to me if you had not shown up. Now again, you have beguiled him. I want you to leave Salzburg and never return."

His intense gaze might have bowled me over but I heard Hansi enter the apartment, kiss his mother hello and exchange a few words, then pushing the door and me out of the way.

"We were just speaking of you, Hans. So good of you to arrive at the perfect moment." Gunther stepped back to look at the lawn and forest.

Hansi looked at me for direction. I shrugged and pointed toward the mountain that Gunther had become, an 'I have no idea' look crinkling my face.

Gunther said, "Don't think for a minute that I don't see those rings. Such clichés."

Hansi puffed his cheeks in exasperation. He walked halfway to Gunther, who turned to us, a tear trickled over his cheek. He dabbed his hanky to catch it.

"I was telling Sam that I never liked him. That I used him. I love you, Hans. I love you. You were both too absorbed in the quaintness of an international love affair to see that I loved you. You have hurt me so." He turned back to the view.

Hansi gave me the same 'I have no idea' look.

He indicated a chair, "Have a seat, Gunther," he swept his hand grandiloquently from the forest to the chair. "May I get you a coffee and pastry? A tipple of Mutti's schnapps?"

Gunther slunk and sat.

"You mock." He mopped his brow and dabbed his tear ducts.

Hansi sat.

"Let's be frank, Gunter, because this theatre is unbecoming. I asked you to not bother my mother again. Yet here you are. This is precisely why I don't like you. You want respect but respect no one. You want to be considered in society but you mock society. You want to be an important player. You throw your weight around. Why would I like a person who is rude, demanding of attention, and disrespectful of others?"

He sat back and waited.

Gunther looked at me.

"I am not oblivious to my faults, dearest Hans. I am not unaware of how I chafe society. I am cognizant that most find me abhorrent. What you don't understand is that I have cultivated this persona because I could not have what I loved. I could not lure you to me through him," he thrust his jaw and arm my direction, "and I could not buy my way into the world that owed me. So I built my empire. I built my cocoon of power. I waited. Until Andreas died. I waited for your return." He looked away from me. "I was sure Sam would never return."

Hansi chuckled. "That's something we shared." It moved neither Gunther nor me. He sniffed the gentle Austrian air in a semblance of apology.

I felt a gentle nudge of the door against my back and was forced to step aside.

"Herr Drecker." Mutti W. stepped onto the patio. "You are a tragic man. Your tragedy is of your own making. No one owes you anything. No one owes you love because you want them to love you. No one owes you respect because you are a successful businessman. Your tragedy is that you never learned to love." She put her hand on Hansi's shoulder. "These two men have loved twice. They have lost once. You are yet a child begging to play with others. I have watched your career for decades. I was impressed with your success. I was repelled by your meddling. Quite frankly, Herr Drecker, you need a good spanking until you see the worth you have. Maybe it is time for you to move to Vienna or Berlin to recreate yourself, as you seem most capable of doing."

She squeezed Hansi's shoulder.

"I must ask you to leave, Herr Drecker. You are welcome back but only when you have grown up."

She touched my hand and smiled when she returned to her chair, tucking herself in. I held the door open.

The quiet of the forest enfolded us. The wait felt terminal but was a minute or less.

"I shall leave you to your lives." Gunther pushed himself up. He walked to the door. Sotto voce he said to me, "Leave. Don't come back. If you do, you will rue the day."

"Pleasure to see you, Gunther," I said.

"Can't resist a good lie, can you Sam Greyling." He minced to the hallway door and closed it with a huff.

We sat next to Mutti W.

"That was fun," she said over the edge of her coffee cup.

We gave her an outline of the reasons for his actions.

"Such a fool," she said.

"Thank you for your words, Adelheid," I warmed her with a smile.

"May I see your rings?" A wry grin chattered across her face. "I assume you were going to tell me until that man appeared. Do you suppose he did that to ruin your announcement."

We agreed with her that must be what happened because we both forgot we needed to tell others of our plans.

"They are quite modern looking, aren't they?"

Hansi said, "The symbol is our choice, Mutti. I love Sam. This is right."

"It is also time, my son," she touched his cheek. "Andreas is your happy past. We all loved him, too. I feared you would be lost in grief. Until my American son returned." She touched my cheek with her other hand. "I always knew this day would come," she sighed back into her chair, dropping her touch and closing her tear-filled eyes. Hansi reached over to catch the tear before it fell from her tired face.

"We love you, Mutti. Thank you for your words. Rest a little before we take you to lunch."

"I forgot to tell them you were coming." She fell into sleep, a smile twitching the corners of her mouth.

We moved to the patio, then took a walk over the lawn to the edge of the forest. We sat on a granite bench looking back at the former convent.

"The prince archbishop built to impress," I said, breaking our silence.

Hansi dropped his head. I put my arm around his shoulders.

"What's the matter?"

His lungs emptied in a great wind. I held my breath.

"They are not hopeful," he whispered.

"What do you mean?"

"I am glad you came back. She may not be here when you return."

"That can't be," I was incredulous. "Something can be done?"

He put his hand on my thigh.

"No medication will stop the clock, mein Schatz. It is age only. I will speak with her. The prince archbishop's convent wants instructions."

"I'll extend my stay."

"Sam, no. You will go home to prepare your return. The sooner you go, the sooner you are back."

"You will not do this alone."

He leaned into me. I engulfed him in my arms. The bird song filtered around us. The fragrance of trees and earth floated over us. The light of midday warmed us.

Hansi unwrapped from our hug.

"Anna Marie must know," he stood, pulling his cell from his trousers. "Get Mutti ready for lunch. I'll join you in a minute." He strode across the lawn toward the front of the building, cursing the lack of bars to make his call.

I did the same, dialing my real estate agent in the States. I expected to leave a message because it was 4 a.m. for him. He picked up. I told him I had to cut my time to two weeks. He said he'd have the staging ready to replace my furniture and would text me his listing for approval. I asked him to find me a large storage unit and to recommend professional packers. In my mind I gave myself ten days because I could do a lot of my financial transactions from here.

I sat next to Mutti until she sensed my presence and opened her eyes.

"Time for lunch?" she said, her strength returning. I helped her up and got her to the bathroom to refresh.

Hansi returned as I helped her with her sweater.

We dined with all eyes on us. Hansi and I smiled at the residents. Mutti ignored them.

She whispered as best she could, "They spend their time comparing their health to others, calculating who will go next." She chuckled through her soup. "You thought they were looking at you? You vainglorious young men." She chortled through her schnitzel. "They wait for St. Nicholas hoping Krampus will touch them gently on the shoulder with one switch. Surviving one more year. One more holiday." She laughed through her strudel.

Catching my eye, she said, "Sam Greyling, if you hurt my son, I will haunt you from the great beyond. Do not take me lightly on this, my American son." Her gaze through her eyebrows chilled me because, even though I didn't believe in an afterlife, I knew what Mutti Wortmann said was what would happen.

I lifted my ring finger and made sure the diamond flashed in her eyes.

"The glare of baubles means nothing, Sam." She touched her breast. "Truth is in the heart."

She sipped her glass of wine and sighed contentment.

Twenty-Three

Le Cordon Bleu called Katarin with an early opening because another student dropped out at the last minute.

We scrambled but got it together. I downloaded a language app to get him started. Anton found a language instructor who agreed to meet Rheinhart and Fred at Gare de l'Est. He would host the boys for a few days until the accommodations came through from the school admissions office.

We stood on the concourse of the Salzburg Hauptbahnhof waiting for the Steiners to arrive with Fred, and the Zechas with Rheinhart. Their train through Stuttgart was to depart in a few minutes.

"Fred will fall in love with Paris," I said.

"The more he experiences the world, the better singer he will be." Hansi, the practical.

"He could get distracted."

"He and Rheinhart could hook up." He looked at me. "It would be good for both of them."

"Mutti and Vatti Steiner would be hurt if he doesn't come back." I stopped pacing.

He stopped looking at the time.

"Greyling," he said, "is there something you are trying to tell me?"

"What do you mean?"

"Cryptic comments about Rheinhart and Fred that sound a lot like you are sending a message."

I looked at the time. "They're going to miss this train."

"There's another one in two hours, same route. You've changed the subject."

I pulled him to sit on the nearest bench.

"What if I change my mind?"

"I'll sell the ring and we'll never see each other again."

"Be serious."

"That's not a threat, Greyling. At some point I have to be practical about it. If you don't come back, I'll alter the Trust, Anders will work with your attorney to make it happen, the jeweler will buy the ring back. I'll marry Fred, or Rheinhart, or Gunther. That would solve that problem, wouldn't it."

"You would not."

"Fred is a lot of fun in bed. Rheinhart must be, too. Gunther and I could come to an arrangement, be companions with benefits. Think of the travel. I'd avoid your side of the U.S. but I'd go everywhere else."

I think he wanted to laugh. Maybe.

"You'll miss too much, Greyling. I know you. If you stay away, you will be miserable."

The commotion coming up the stairs couldn't be ignored.

Quick greetings and goodbyes.

I slipped the friendship ring into Rheinhart's hand. "A token to keep you honest," I said.

"No ceremony?" He smiled and kissed my cheeks three times.

The boys loaded onto the train. We waved it off and told the Steiners we'd walk to their home for lunch. Herr Zecha would be there. We said we'd get a dessert and after lunch digestif.

Walking out of the station we both received texts telling us thanks for everything. They felt final, like we'd never see them again. We decided we had become the worst kind of worrying parents and that they were caught up in their adventures, not realizing that worrying parents don't need teasing, unclear texts.

We had an hour or so to make our way to the Steiners.

I made Hansi promise he wouldn't tell anyone then I dragged him to the Bastion to the dwarf garden.

"I used to come here as a kid," he said. "I never think of it now."

He tucked his arm around my waist. Secure. Wanted. Needed. Maybe. What do I know.

"Many angstisch afternoons for me. Worrying about school and if we'd be caught, and I'd be sent home. If any of my friends had followed me, I would have had to find another quiet place."

He twirled me into a hug. Warm and tender. His breath on my neck.

"This is our place now," he whispered. "I want to take you here. In the middle of the grass." He pulled me to the spot where I had eaten my sandwich a few weeks before.

"Keep off the grass," I pointed at the sign. "It's still morning, mein Hertz. It can wait."

He changed direction and pulled me to the bench. We sat encircling each other with a huge hug.

"Which dwarf is your favorite?" The wet of his tongue coursed up my neck.

"It depends on the day and my mood," I said. His soft, thick hair swept through my hand.

He waited.

"Feeling a bit like the troll," I twittered in a not-so-trollischer whine.

"I thought you'd say the Bier Mädchen." He laughed and poked my ribs.

"You?"

"Has to be the Wanderer."

We marched around like kids taking selfies with each one, capturing our great mood.

We were late to the Steiners.

Herr Zecha sat patiently on the sofa—stiff, stern. Was he really younger than me?

Mutti und Vatti fussed creating a simple lunch, knowing Zecha was the master chef but tittering that they had learned a thing or two in their travels.

"Fred will help Rheinhart acclimate to Paris," I said, receiving a taciturn scold from Herr Zecha and a nod of agreement from Vatti S.

"They are fine young men," Mutti S. added, buttering her brioche, which I thought was excessive gilding of the batter. She taunted me with the butter plate.

Herr Zecha broke his silence. "Thank you, Herr Wortmann and Herr Greyling, for helping my son find his way."

"It remains to be seen if he has found anything," I said. Hansi black-and-blued my shin in a swift kick. I corrected course. "You graciously allowing him the time to study with the best, will make your endeavors more successful."

Hansi stroked my smarting shin, adding to the discomfort.

"We will be at Restaurant Zecha this evening," Hansi reminded the table. "My farewell dinner for Sam."

Muti S. added, "Perhaps we should make a reservation to celebrate his return in a few weeks?" She raised her wine in toast, "To happy successes and happier returns."

Vatti S. said, "Frederic must return soon also because the date for his recital is approaching. I hope he practices with the voice instructor he has for a day in Paris."

"They will both be fine," Hansi said. "Fred needed a break. Helping Rheinhart get settled will be good for both of them." I wondered if my shin was bleeding. He should have removed his shoes when we arrived, like the rest of us. 'Schue aus' was the rule after all.

I shifted in my chair to reach for more of something and escape the leg torture. Mutti S. patted my hand away, "Manners, Sam."

I wanted to rat on Hansi and his 'schue aus' defiance. He had such an angelic grin on his face that I couldn't out him. She knew anyway.

"Thank you each for your kindnesses these past few weeks." Hansi raised his glass. "To your support and your encouragements."

Glasses were refilled. We chatted about what had been accomplished. We laughed at fortunate coincidences and unexpected obstacles.

Herr Zecha broke the convivial mood.

"I have a restaurant to run." He bowed with polite Austrian manners.

Mutti S. smiled my way and I pointed down at Hansi's shoes. She winked.

On our way back to Getreidegasse we did a loop past Augies, through Neutor and the tunnel, then into Altstadt. We stopped at the horse fountain and I nearly fell in retrieving trash from an American coffee chain. Hansi said something rude yet appropriate about cultural domination by an ancient civilization. Sarcasm danced in the fountain and splashes of water.

A horse carriage full of overly loud Americans, of all things, stopped to snap their pictures, and the horses dropped some berries as they rested. One pale-faced, dark haired young man focused on us and so we obliged with fondling and kissing. He laughed and snapped away until an older man jerked him to look at the castle. He waved goodbye as the carriage made its way toward Stift St. Peter's and Dom Platz, the end of the road for tourists.

"You will miss this place," Hansi dropped his own berry between us.

"Don't, Hansi, not after a good day."

"Inevitable," he took my hands in his.

"What's inevitable is that we are getting married."

"I have decided to treasure the ring. It's only worth what I get for it. An investment, of sorts."

"Why are you doing this?"

"I know you, mein Schatz. It would seem—still better than you know yourself."

"Stop teasing, Hansi."

"Preparing myself for the inevitable, Greyling."

"You don't trust what I say," I withdrew one hand and dropped it into the cool water. Eddies formed behind my fingers as I swished. "We created a Fund with our names on it. Is that not worth my promise?"

"You will get distracted. You will find excuses. You will slow time down until there is no decision to be made because you use time as a distraction and then as an excuse."

"Enough, Hansi, mein Hertz," I said, lifting his chin, feeling the coarseness of his midday beard. I stroked his jaw then leaned in to kiss him. He pulled back.

"I won't apologize anymore for the past," I stood.

"This isn't about the past, Sam. I want a future with you. You are still unsure. Even with these," he touched his ring, the diamond shone in the midday sun.

I put my ring next to his hand.

"These mean something, Hansi," I pushed our hands together so our rings touched. "The minute we put them on they meant commitment. Honesty. Honor. Love. Forever. They don't work if you put it on without those things. They don't work on two continents. Apart. Mine doesn't come off until you plant me under some tree on some mountain."

He withdrew his hand.

"They don't work if you don't trust me," I pushed against him. He nearly fell into the fountain.

"Time for a nap?" I suggested.

We walked to Castle Getreidegasse, silent.

When we awoke from the true nap – the kind without sex, intimacy, holding, kissing – I said, "Should I cancel Zecha? I can stay out by the airport tonight. It's an early flight. I'm OK with that if that is better."

"You need a shower."

"What do you need, mein Hertz?" Sadness.

"A shower. Get moving."

"Hansi, come with me to the States."

"Nice try," he chucked a snark my way. "I can't leave Mutti to Anna Marie. Anders wants to work on the Trust. I may have tenants on Neutorstrasse I need to deal with."

"Sure. Makes sense."

I stripped and ran the water to warm it.

As I made to step into the shower tub, he was behind me. I panicked. "What are you doing?"

"Giving you a reason to come back." He licked my shoulders, my nipples danced to his touch, the hairs on my neck stood firm. I felt him firm between my legs.

"Get in," he said, nudging my butt with his dick.

He shifted us under the steaming water. His hands brushed my back and butt. He reached around to massage my chest and gut. Pleasure rumbled between my shoulder blades. He licked and nipped my flesh and waited for me to catch up. He paused to let my sadness and grief wash off me.

It didn't wash away. It welled into my eyes and my sinuses and my throat. I cried my fear and my lies and my grief for Thomas and my happiness for Hansi. I cried it all into the stream of steaming water.

Hansi held me tight, supporting my weak knees. He made sure I knew he was there.

He grabbed my hands away from the shower wall and pulled them close to my body, holding me fast against his. The diamonds in our rings touched. Flowing through the water was sparkle, light, and brilliance.

I twisted to face him, making sure we didn't slip into the tub.

"I love you, Hansi. Mein Hertz. Forever."

He urged my mouth open with his tongue, assuring me of his love, caressing my body. He moved slowly. Flashes of our first time decades ago. I responded in kind to every pressure, every nuance, every tweak and twist of pleasure.

After long enough for the water pressure to subside and the wet to feel tepid, we completed our love making. Glorious and full.

As we soaped up, I said, "I need a nap."

He washed my dick and balls, squeezing a little too hard after our hour of exercise.

"Sorry," he offered. "We have to get to Zecha. You need to pack. Get moving."

"Yes, Gunther."

He slapped my ass as I squeegeed the wet from my body.

"Don't even go there, Herr Greyling."

We grabbed a twenty-minute nap wrapped in each other's arms.

We primped into suits, somehow ending up with ties of matching color but different design. There was no time to change.

It was strange to not have Rheinhart serving our table. Herr Zecha created a sumptuous five-course extravaganza with white truffle amuse-bouches, barley and late onion consommés, wild boar with black truffle and black currant compote with new red potatoes and broccoli hearts, mixed green salad drizzled with sesame oil, and a triple-apple strudel with honey, whipped cream, and raspberry coulis drizzle. Wine pairings for each course, finished with forty-year single malts, and a champagne toast served to all guests in our honor. We staggered back toward Castle Getreidegasse through a nearly empty Altstadt – the way we liked it.

Hunkered down on the edge of the composer's statue in Mozartplatz was the young American tourist, down in the dumps and sulking. He saw us and waved his American charm. We approached, weaving slightly.

"English?" he queried.

"If you are going to visit a country," I said, "you might want to learn a few phrases in the lingua franca." We teased him. His shy demeaner was inviting, adding to our intoxication.

"Should we?" I said to Hansi.

The youth looked hopeful and daunted, panting with expectation.

"The best bar in town is across the footbridge just down there. Cross the road then up the slope. If you step onto cobbles, you have gone too far. Look for the rainbow flag above the last door on the left. They'll take care of you there. Tell them Fred sent you. That'll get their attention."

We turned to leave, feeling smug that we may have started an affair with Salzburg.

"Which one of you is Fred?" he asked.

"Neither," we shouted in unison. "But he's the talk of the town and will be famous one day. Enjoy Salzburg."

Twenty-Four

My flight was moved to noon, which was good because I hadn't finished packing the night before. We had time for breakfast, which still felt rushed. I fussed that my connection in Frankfurt would be tight what with going through immigration and back through security.

I didn't know that Hansi had invited half of Salzburg to say goodbye and to remind me that I had a family waiting for my return. Built-in love. Built-in pressure. Built-in I wasn't sure what else. I would have preferred an intimate peck on the cheek and quick hug from Hansi before venturing into the efficient, no nonsense Austrian security apparatus.

Surreal didn't capture it.

Balloons in every color but black. A banner saying 'goodbye / welcome home'. People gawking as if someone in our gathering was famous. A few older folks recognized the Steiners who dawdled from the parking garage to join in the festivities.

"No oompah send off?" I smiled at Hansi.

"They all wanted to say farewell."

"That sounds too final."

"Hedging our bets," he bumped my shoulder. "You have a history."

"Once. Once I didn't return. What will it take?" I smiled but its weakness radiated nothing to Hansi. He curled a smile my way.

Anna Marie and Anders pushed Mutti W. in a wheelchair into the center of the group. She beamed her excitement, perhaps more about being away from Castle Wortmann than to see her wayward American son off to lands far away.

I watched the big clock flip numerals faster than I wanted. I calculated if I could do all I needed to by phone and internet. There were too many memories stashed in boxes in closets, the basement, the attic, and in my home office. My ten-day time limit to turn this around was tight but doable.

Hansi squeezed my hand to bring me back to goodbyes.

"What if I rented the house? It would be a source of income. I could rent it furnished and stuffed with my stuff."

"Let me count," Hansi said, "first, second, or third barrier to returning?"

"Letting go of a life in thirty days is a fast turnaround." He didn't know I had put more pressure on myself. I accepted that I might have to relax into it.

"Thinking of options." I brushed his hand.

"Do that on the plane, mein Schatz."

Mutti Steiner brought mini-strudels and champagne in forever tumblers to hide it from the culture cops.

"There's a marketing idea," I said, leaning in for a peck on the cheek.

"We will have a big celebration when you return. There are many people who want to meet you." She handed me a strudel on a plate with a paper napkin and wooden fork. The pre-flight hostess with manners. "Frederic will be back. We will present an intimate concert in your honor." She pulled me back close to her face. "You know, I am still in touch with some of Andreas' spy friends. They will find you if I give them the word. My promise to you." She let me go with a smile.

What the fuck was I to make of that? I took it as a bit of well-practiced humor. The twinkle in her eye bounced between love and menace, or so it seemed. I laughed, feeding my face with her superior strudels. More than one. Binge eating menace and love. The champagne tickled my mouth and washed my throat. All the better to chat with.

Mutti W. pulled a present from the wheelchair. I leaned down to accept it with pecks to both cheeks, and a third tender endearment to her forehead.

"It is so you will write to tell us when you are returning," she smiled triumph and the same impishness of the dwarves at Mirabell Gardens. "Open it. You will have time to write on the plane."

Lovely pink stationery with edelweiss and roses for a border. A stack of paper with matching envelopes from an era gone by. "Frau Wortmann," I chuckled at her with my hand out to stop her protestations. "Adelheid—you shouldn't have. I will write as frequently as I can."

She beamed delight.

I leaned over to Hansi. "Text me the address of Castle Wortmann. Obligations are piling up."

Our chortle was cut short by a violin playing that song from that movie that mirrored the gift stationery. Tourists stopped to listen and smile. A few sang along. When the tune melted into the rafters, she played a Mozart sonata for solo violin. Somber, slow, moving, exquisite.

"You had to hear me play one more time in your life, Uncle Sam," she said as the air floated her final notes throughout the concourse. Applause wafted from various nooks and crannies and knots of travelers.

"Anna Marie, you have touched me more than I can say," I said.

"If you come back, you'll hear more," she hugged me long and hard. "Don't hurt my brother and mother again," she breathed against my ear. Her smile returned as she pulled away. The smile didn't match the darkness of her gaze.

I got the point. Come back or die. At least I had options.

The party wound down when the numbers on the clock struck 10:00 a.m.

"Security beckons," I said, with a round of hugs for everyone.

Except Hansi.

He said, "I'll walk you there."

"It's just over there," I pointed 40 meters along the way. A line had formed. I needed to get in it.

"It's a small airport, Greyling."

Anders handed balloons to passing kids. Anna Marie got the banner down somehow. She rolled it up lowering her brow into that darkness. "Safe travels, Uncle Sam." She smiled.

"Thank you for the concert. I look forward to many more." I shot her my happy grin. She winced, or was it a wink. What do I know.

I assured the Steiners I would be in touch about the Trust, Fred, and Rheinhart. I thanked them like I was never coming back. They looked pained but resigned, much like Hansi. It was more than obvious they had discussed the possibility I would dial in from the States to fulfill my commitments.

"I will see you in a few weeks. We can stream some calls. It won't be long." I was determined to be determined.

Hansi stopped me fifteen feet from the line into security. The numbers on the clock flipped too soon.

"You are loved here, mein Schatz, my Greyling." He hugged me hard. I returned the same. "All I ask is that you be honest with your actions." He stepped back, hands held up flat between us defending himself from my frustration.

I leaned in and kissed his luscious lips.

"I will text you my journey. We can stream later. Nine-hour difference, don't forget. Your evening is my morning. My late evening is your morning. We'll figure it out."

"I love you, Samuel Scott Greyling. Do not forget that. Ever."

"Mein Hertz. My Hansi."

We pecked cheeks then lip locked one last time.

Just before entering the airlock of security, I looked back. There was no one to wave to. They had all gone.

Except.

Turning from the window that looked toward Untersberg, Gunther raised his hand in salute, not goodbye.

What was I to do with that?

Acknowledgements

This story, and ones to follow, germinated when I was a university student studying in Salzburg, Austria. There are many known and unknown influences on the development of *Hansi & Greyling.*

Characters in the story are an amalgam of many people and citizens of Salzburg whom I met as a student. There are no intended likenesses to specific individuals but there are inferences from their influence of my becoming a citizen of the world. A few specifics will remain anonymous for personal reasons.

I wish to thank the people of Salzburg from my student days in the early 1970s. Your kindness toward this student helped me understand the world from varying perspectives. I became a better person and human being because of you. I wish to thank the residents of Salzburg today for allowing my story to be told within their lovely and gorgeous environment. Any misrepresentations are rightly laid at my feet. Your city is inspiring in beauty and in people. Your bier is outstanding and fortifying. Your music defines a world of excellence and joy.

My gratitude is extensive for my friends and family who encouraged, supported, and took the time to read a few lines here and there. The feedback I received helped me craft a better story and clarify the characters whom I have grown to love.

Dave Zine and Marlise Stroebe, Kenda-Lee Gaynham, and Deirdre Crowley have been particularly supportive. Larry Whitson and Patrick Alexander laughed with me through the rough patches. Larry's feedback after his read through helped immensely. George Lewis listened and encouraged. Kirk Bell's comments focused my writing on specifics that enlarged a few characters. Monte and Margaret Nugent were supportive and encouraging throughout.

I learned a great deal from Sue Fitzmaurice of Rebel Magic Books, my editor and publisher. Her online course was inspiring. Her editing, suggestions and support were invaluable. Knowing Sue was behind me kept me focused and moving from page to page in rewrites and edits. Thank you.

My greatest thanks and praise go to the many men I met in Salzburg on Friday nights at our pub on the Steingasse. Those conversations on politics, philosophy, and social justice inspired me even when I relied on bier to get me through my meager German speaking skills. Our laughter filled the pub. Our indignation at the state of the world darkened our moods. It was a heady, inspiring, and lovely time. Well remembered.

The seed for this novel was planted when my roommate in Salzburg introduced me to a gentleman two days before our group left Salzburg at the end of our year of study. It took decades and life circumstances to blossom. The seed grew into the question that inspires much of my writing: 'What if.' What if the man I met decades ago had been the one. There is no regret in the asking but a simple sense of wonder and gratitude about what might have happened had I met this now unknown man at the beginning of my year of study in Salzburg, Austria.

About the Author

Timothy Nugent is an American writer living in Norwich, England. *Hansi & Greyling* is his first novel, and is the opening of a series with the same characters. He has written for traditional and social media, produced and published plays, and written short stories. He was born and raised in Montana, lived in four states and three countries, and prides himself on being a citizen of the world.

REBEL
MAGIC
BOOKS

www.rebelmagicbooks.com

Printed in Great Britain
by Amazon

36277592R00148